Your Next Chapter

Dream It. Design It. Live It.

Your Next Chapter

Dream It. Design It. Live It.

How To Live A Purposeful Life Without Limitations

CHRISTINE L. STALLARD

UNSTOPPABLE
PUBLISHING

Library of Congress Control Number: 2021904113

Print ISBN: 978-1-7358589-3-7
E-book ISBN: 978-1-7358589-4-4

Unstoppable Publishing
231 Public Square, Suite 300
Franklin, Tennessee 37064

Cover Design by Jessica Tookey
Cover Photography by Christine L. Stallard
Interior Layout by Janell E. Robisch, Speculations Editing
Photography by Keith Ross, Keith's Frame of Mind

DISCLAIMER

This is a work of nonfiction. The content provided in this book
is intended to be used only as a source of helpful information of a general nature on the subjects discussed, not as a
substitute for consulting with experts including medical professionals. If such level of assistance is required, the services
of a competent professional should be sought. Neither the
author nor the publisher shall be liable or responsible for any
loss, claim, or damage allegedly arising from any information or suggestion in this book. References are provided for
informational purposes only and do not constitute endorse-
ment of any websites or other sources. The author cannot be
held accountable for the information provided by, or actions
resulting from, accessing these resources.

Printed in the United States of America

This book is dedicated to the ones I love.

A Gift for You ||||

Your Next Chapter Companion Journal

(Retails for $39.95...My gift to you!)

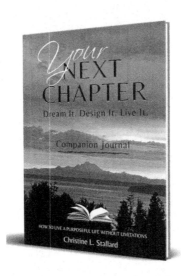

Get the PDF version of the companion journal to *Your Next Chapter* for free.

The exercises in the book and companion journal are tools designed especially for you. Use them to write your next chapter so you can live on purpose and by design instead of by default.

To access your gift...

1. Visit https://nextchapterbook.com/gift
2. Tell us where to email your access link
3. Check your email to download your companion journal
4. As you read this book, use your journal to complete the exercises and make notes

Contents |||

Foreword ‖

I'll never forget the day that I met Christine Stallard for the first time. We were at the Unstoppable Influence Inner Circle retreat, and after a warm hug, she let everyone know that we could call her "Christy" because that's what her friends call her. Everyone in the room immediately was at ease and felt a connection to this kind soul who had recently joined our group.

As I got to know Christy better, I discovered that she had an incredible backstory. One that took her on a journey to the top of a male-dominated industry. It was so inspiring to hear how this wise and warm woman was able to break through the glass ceiling, defy the odds, and earn the respect and admiration of many in the process. Yet even more inspiring than her corporate success was watching Christy navigate the next three years as she began writing her own "next chapter" as a retired corporate executive.

Christy went all-in to the process of redesigning her life in a way that felt authentic to her. She not only invested countless hours and dollars in tools that would help her grow in this new arena, she also did something most people don't—she took what she was learning and put it into action.

As a result of her efforts, she cracked the code and found a fulfilling path after retiring from her career. Now she's helping others do the same with this book, her personal coaching, and Next Chapter programs.

Navigating life after a major transition can be messy. Really messy. I know, because I've been there. And while there is certainly beauty in the mess, the process doesn't have to be painful, and dare I say that it can actually be enjoyable!

That's what Christine Stallard does in *Your Next Chapter*. She takes the mystery out of life after a transition and provides easy-to-follow action steps that will help you write the pages of your next chapter, whatever that may be.

Life wasn't meant to be lived by default, only living for the approval of others. It is a blank canvas that we get to design. We are in the driver's seat!

Oprah Winfrey once said: "Your journey begins with a choice to get up, step out, and live fully."

Now is the time to start living your very best life. You couldn't ask for a better guide for your journey than Christine Stallard—raw and vulnerable yet strong, confident, and wise.

I believe that we are all here on purpose and for a purpose. There is no coincidence that you are reading this book right now. There is something beautiful waiting for you in these pages.

Congratulations on taking this all-important first step to designing your best life! I am excited for the lives you will touch as you step into your purpose and write your own next chapter.

Natasha Hazlett
Author, *Unstoppable Influence:
Be You. Be Fearless. Transform Lives.*

"And suddenly you know: It's time to start something new and trust the magic of beginnings."

— Meister Eckhart,
German Dominican theologian, writer

Once Upon A Time |||

My Transition

It's amazing what can get piled on you in just 24 months. I was under a mandatory evacuation order for five weeks as a wildfire raged to within two miles of my dream home. Not long after, we sold our property and lived out of boxes for 10 months until we could find and move into our next home. As if that wasn't enough, around the same time I lost two of my beloved canine family members within four months of each other.

Major life transitions are very personal and can be devastating. A divorce, move, retirement, and loss of a job or loved one are common ones that many of us face at some point.

This one totally rocked my world.

And, it all started when I walked out of the corporate world.

For 30 years, I had been an official spokesperson, senior-level executive, department manager, and trusted advisor. I sat on numerous industry trade association boards, designed award-winning marketing materials, wrote a history book, managed employees and projects, communicated complex issues through a variety of means, and developed grassroots networks and support for industry issues.

To say I was deeply rooted in the industry would be an understatement.

I was passionate about and proud of the work I was doing. Unfortunately, I had allowed my corporate career to define who I was. Other people's thoughts and opinions of me became my truth. I wasn't prepared for a life that didn't include the corporate identity I had come to know, love, and rely upon.

When I walked out the door for the last time, my world drastically changed.

I felt lost, empty, and forgotten.

One of my roles as an organizational leader and coach was to counsel employees preparing for retirement or a career move. Often confused and emotional about the decision they were about to make, I assured them it was normal for employees to come and go. The organization would adjust and move on and so would they. Change was not only okay, it was healthy.

But now my organization and my work world had moved on without me, and it was time for me to take my own advice. What seemed easy to give was not so easy to take. Go figure!

The idea of looking at my life story as a book with chapters and pages didn't occur to me until I was in the thick of that transition when I finally realized my life wasn't over, only a chapter of my book, my story, was.

It was simply time for me to turn the page.

Starting a new chapter may sound exciting, but for me, it meant taking a giant step outside my comfort zone. Inside that zone, life was on autopilot and most everything seemed familiar and predictable. I knew what I was good at, what brought me joy, and what would cause anxiety and stress. For the most part, I knew how to manage my emotions and reactions. I felt in control.

But in reality, I wasn't.

Other people and circumstances had filled the pages of my book, and because I allowed that to happen, I had given up control. I was living life by default instead of by design. Don't get me wrong—I have been blessed with a loving family, an amazing circle of friends, and a highly successful, rewarding career filled with exceptional colleagues. I am forever grateful for the people who influence and enrich my life.

But the circumstances of living life by default had definitely taken its toll. When I looked in the mirror, I really wasn't sure who was staring back at me. She resembled the confident, competent woman who had accomplished more than most in a world still dominated by men, but she looked so stressed out, tired, and sad. Leaving the corporate world without a plan had shaken my confidence, and it showed. But why?

Now I had no more alarm clock waking me out of a sound sleep at 5:00 am four days a week. No more daily commute in all kinds of inclement weather and treacherous road conditions. No structured workday with start and end times and meetings and appointments filling my calendar. No projects, deadlines, employees, or crises to manage. And no more trading my time for the amount of money someone else said I was worth.

"What could be better?" I asked myself. I now had the freedom to stay up as late as I wanted without worrying about the alarm clock, the option of staying safe in my home instead of braving the winter storms to commute to work, and the freedom to plan my day based on what was important to me, not to someone else.

As much as I tried to convince myself this new life was exciting, I felt lifeless.

And because you're reading this book, I suspect we're kindred spirits on this topic.

Many of us allow ourselves to be defined by someone or something else. It may be our corporate careers, our children or grandchildren, our significant others, our hobbies, or our community involvement. We get so wrapped up in who we think we are in relation to the outside world that we forget to pay attention to who we are deep down inside—even when we're all by ourselves.

We allow our thoughts and dreams to get drowned out, when in reality, it's our dreams and who we are when we're all by ourselves that really should matter. My life transition made me realize that the time I spent in the corporate world had defined me to the point I had buried who I really was.

I had allowed that to happen, but now was the perfect time to rediscover the real me.

I knew that I wasn't done contributing and serving others. And while my ego tried to convince me I was too old, I knew deep down that my life experiences could help me rediscover my passion and inspire other women to live their lives by design as well.

So one day, after spending an entire Sunday in bed feeling sorry for myself, I decided enough was enough. Time to pull myself out of the state I was in and move on. No one else was going to do it for me; it was all up to me. And I was ready.

The first step was to get out of my own way, quit dwelling on the past, and face my fear of the unknown. Once I did, I started reading every self-improvement book I could lay my hands on and listened to meditation tapes and podcasts. I started a new business venture in direct sales, hired a brilliant business coach, and surrounded myself with uplifting, dynamic, and positive women.

During this time, something else struck me. If living life by design meant following your dreams, living in alignment with your truth, and living on purpose, then it would make sense to start with an assessment of where and who you are today, uncover and understand your truth, and figure out what living on purpose would look like in your future.

Aha! That's how I can begin to rediscover the real me.

But wait just a damn minute...I've done this before!

In my corporate life, it was called strategic planning. Organizations use this process to identify strengths, weaknesses, opportunities, and threats. The analysis is used to define the organization's values, vision, mission, and strategic initiatives, and uncover areas that need attention. The plan becomes a guide and a tool to define the organization's future, keep it on track, and measure success.

With all the brilliance of Einstein, I asked myself, "Why not apply the same concepts on a personal level to get the same results, and coach others to do it as well so they can also live a life of passion and purpose?"

It begins with unpackaging your story.

Each one of us has a story. Each one is unique, and each one matters. Wanting or considering a career move or staring at an open door to a new chapter is the perfect time to pause and reflect on who you are, where you are in your life story, and where you want to be in the next chapter.

The planning you do now will uncover your dreams, knowledge, experience, and uniqueness that will define your perfect path to tomorrow. It's your foundation for living life by design.

I know it can be done because I've done it. I learned so much in this life transition, including how to trust myself and trust that God had a plan for me that would unfold on His timing, making my life better than I ever imagined it could be.

The *Next Chapter Plan*™ and this book are my gifts to you. They are my way of sharing my experience to ensure that you too can confidently navigate any life transition.

Your Transition

Every end is also a beginning. But we tend to forget this when we're facing fear of the unknown or feeling a loss. We focus, understandably, on what we leave behind instead of getting excited about what might lie ahead.

I get it. It's tricky when you don't know what the future holds for you tomorrow or next week. But I challenge you to channel that uncertainty and fear into positive energy. Know that you can do it. Trust yourself. The perfect next chapter exists, if you are only willing to look at things a little differently or to walk down a new path.

Instead of asking yourself "Why me?" ask "What's next?" That will put you in the right mindset to be creative, to dream and design your ideal future. And if you're asking what's next, you'll be nudging yourself to take action and make the changes you need to feel better about yourself.

Start with your stories, because they contribute to who you are today. Peel back the layers of your onion and get to the heart of who you really are without all the untruths and labels that have clouded your truth, sometimes for years. Identify and tear off the masks you put on to protect yourself from what others may see or think about you.

Then...

- Develop the right mindset.
- Uncover your likes and dislikes.
- Map out your journey, but be flexible along the way.
- Journal your thoughts to help you gain clarity.
- Apply your current skills in ways that add value to others.

You must do these things if you're going to dream, design, and live your next chapter. But that also means you'll be stepping outside your comfortable, normal world into the unknown.

That fear of the unknown is what stops most of us dead in our tracks. It almost stopped me.

That's normal. But you can learn to face those fears. Push through them. Recognize your unique skills and learn new ones. Understand what you're capable of doing. Because once you do that, you're well on your way to living the life of your dreams by design.

With a habit and mindset of asking what's next, you'll get excited about following your dreams. You won't let limiting beliefs define you and your best life.

While you're on this journey, you'll be looking for the message in the mess. Sometimes, the mess *is* the message, if you can believe that! My message was that if I had purposefully designed my next chapter, I could have saved myself a lot of heartache and pushed through it a whole lot more gracefully than I did. I'm not the same person I was at 20, 30, 40, or even 50. My dreams and aspirations are different. I get that now.

So on this journey, you must also be comfortable with where you are and how you've evolved. Some people know what they want to do at an early age, and they go for it. I can think of a few musicians, actors, artists, and authors I would put in that category. But the vast majority of people have no clue.

Pay attention and get comfortable with "the pivot." One or more opportunities will undoubtedly come.

One Last Thought Before You Read On

You'll benefit from reading the book cover to cover, as each section builds on the lessons and exercises from the one before.

- In **Section I: Dream It**, you'll learn about how your mind works and how you can train it to uncover your truth, desires, and dreams.

- In **Section II: Design It**, you'll map out your future life using a proprietary process I developed based on my professional background and experiences.
- Once you know where you want to go, in **Section III: Live It**, you'll learn how to make it come to life.

Each chapter contains an exercise intended to help you take the concepts and turn them into the personal actions—the steps—you'll take on this journey. It will be helpful to write them out in the companion journal. If you didn't grab your copy of the journal, you still have time to do that so you have all your work in one place. At the very least, jot down your thoughts and complete the exercises at the end of the chapters. Make sure you take time to reflect on and complete the exercises I've designed especially for you. They will keep things in perspective on your journey.

Now if you're ready, I want to be your guide to help you design your next and best chapter. All I ask is that you trust yourself and the process. Allow yourself to learn, grow, evolve, and pivot if necessary.

You are the author of your life's story. Your reality is the present, the right now. But your reality can be rewritten. Not only can you do it...you deserve it.

You're one decision away.

SECTION I

Dream It

Chapter 1
Make A Decision

*W*ork gives meaning to our lives. It influences who we are and improves our feelings of self-worth. Being passionate about and good at what you do isn't just something that benefits the organization you work for; it's a gift you give yourself. You have the power to mold your life around your work or find work that supports a lifestyle you've created.

Will you live to work or work to live? Only you can decide.

If you are a woman who is considering or has been thrown into a major life transition, who is seeking a new purpose now that the children are grown or fulfillment after a relationship has changed, or who thought you had no options but to stay in a job you hate until retirement, this book will provide the clarity and confidence you need to shape your future.

There's no better time.

The workforce rules of engagement are changing. Again. But look at where we've been and how we've evolved in terms of industrial revolutions.

The first one made the shift from a reliance on animals and human effort to the use of fossil fuels and mechanical power. The second brought major breakthroughs in the form of electricity distribution, communication (wireless and wired), and new forms of energy generation. The next revolution founded the development of digital systems, communication, and computer advancement, which completely changed how we generated, processed, and shared information.

The current one makes us even more reliant on digital markets and, with that, a shift in the traditional business models to ones that embrace this new hyperconnected world.

Why is this pertinent? Each era disrupted our economic, political, and societal lives as we knew them. We saw significant changes within business, government, media, and society in general.

It's happening now.

The World Economic Forum predicts that the relative power between governments and citizens will be disrupted due to the use of digital communication, and social media will play a critical role in allowing political activists and new movements to influence public policy.

Complex problem solving, critical thinking, and people management will be essential in this industrial revolution. The labor force will need to become more creative as they deal with new products, new technologies, and new ways of working.

Consider the generational differences. Traditional workers born between 1925 and 1945 are dedicated, hard-working, tactful, loyal, and usually trained on the job. They were shaped by the Great Depression, World War II, radio, and movies. Any skills learned were to benefit the company, not the individual. Traditionalists believe that age equals seniority, and they typically stayed with one company until retirement.

Baby Boomers, born between 1946 and 1964, are often workaholics who allow their jobs or careers to define their self-worth. They are competitive, but also motivated by working with a team toward a particular goal. The Vietnam War and the

Civil Rights Movement helped shape them. Their skills are an ingredient of their personal success, and they're more likely to work for more than one company on their path to retirement.

Generation X workers, born between 1965 and 1980, want more of a work/life balance, desire structure and direction, and want to work smarter instead of putting in long hours. They were shaped by the AIDs epidemic, the fall of the Berlin Wall, and the dot-com boom. Often putting their professional interests ahead of the company's, they are more resistant to change at work (especially if it affects their personal lives) and more likely to move on if they feel their place of employment isn't meeting their needs. They learn new skills because they believe that the more they know, the better chance they have of landing a new and better job.

Shaped by Columbine, 9/11, and the internet, Generation Y (Millennials), born between 1981 and 2000 are ambitious and competitive. They desire a fun work/life balance, aren't afraid to question authority, often put family over work, and are typically looking for the next, more intriguing venture.

People born after 2000 are part of Generation Z which was shaped by life after 9/11, the Great Recession, and technology they were introduced to at an early age and have used ever since. They are more creative, independent, and entrepreneurial.

As Baby Boomers retire from corporate jobs, companies are replacing them. But the problem is that most major corporations still operate under a traditional hierarchical business model that has been used for decades and has roots in manufacturing. The younger generations have vastly different work ethics and expectations for how they trade time for money. They are setting new expectations and trends, and questioning and challenging the status quo.

In addition, the expectation of going to school, landing a job that becomes a career, and retiring to pursue full-time leisure is also changing. Yes workers are living longer, but that doesn't mean they are staying in the same workplace or career more than the traditional amount of time. Some continue to work out of necessity, and some work after retirement age to stay connected and because they enjoy the engagement. But the idea that they'll extend their time in the corporate world to meet their financial or emotional needs is fading as an option.

They are tired of contributing to someone else's dream. They want more.

These people are redefining the traditional work environment. They are no longer willing to check the boxes from school to higher education to a career to retirement. No longer content to sit at their desks like zombies during the day and in their living rooms as couch potatoes at night, or willing to live life according to someone else's design, a life by default.

Because you're reading this book and find yourself here, chances are you feel the same way, regardless of your age or generation.

Regardless of where you are in life, it's a perfect time to explore options. Let's get started.

Chapter 2
Rekindle Your Flame ▌▌▌

J've often wondered why some people pursue their dreams with a passion and others don't. I think it comes down to fear. The ones who don't are afraid they can't turn their imagination into reality. They rationalize, justify, and persuade themselves to make decisions that are sensible and comfortable and put on a mask to hide their fear of taking a risk, or worse, of failure.

What are some common masks? Glad you asked!

Mask #1: "I'm too young/ too old to change."

At the age of 23, Evan Spiegel turned down a $3 billion cash acquisition offer from Facebook for Snapchat, the app Spiegel had cofounded with Bobby Murphy two years earlier. What if he had waited, thinking he was too young to do something so ambitious?

Before Vera Wang became one of the world's most famous bridal and fashion designers, she was a competitive figure skater, a journalist (with a degree in art history), a fashion editor, and an accessories design director. At the age of 40, she was planning her own wedding, and that's when she entertained the idea of being a bridal fashion designer—a career that required an entirely different skillset. She did that because of the lack of chic bridal options available at the time, and she was frustrated. What if she had thought she was too old to influence the fashion industry?

Mask #2: "I'm waiting for the perfect time to pursue my dreams."

There really is no perfect time. If you keep waiting, nothing will happen. I say that someday isn't a day at all. Everyone has the same 24 hours in a day. If you make your dreams a priority and you pursue them with passion, you'll find the time. Then when you're looking back on your life, you'll have no regrets about how you spent your time.

Mask #3: "I was told that my dreams were silly and unrealistic."

While listening to advice is often helpful (that's just doing your research), it's your choice whether you file it away or act on it.

Truth is, we do everything for a reason. How our life turns out is largely a product of the choices we make, even if we're not consciously aware that we're making them. Your friends and family mean well and likely have your best interests at heart. But they won't regret for one minute any decision you make in your life; they're too busy regretting ones they have made in their own.

Your dreams are yours alone. Don't let anyone rob you of them. (Unless of course you're out to cause someone harm or you're formulating a plan that will land you in jail. Then by all means, listen to the people in your life who are trying to protect you from yourself.)

So get past all those excuses. It's time to get to work.

First you have to really know yourself—not the self you allow the world to see, but the you who is hidden in every nook and cranny of your soul.

You may be cringing right now because you've spent years hiding the real you from others. You're afraid of what they may think, of being judged or criticized. You're afraid you won't measure up to their standards. Or that maybe (perish the thought) they won't even want to be your friend anymore, on social media or in person.

I get it. I've been there many times, and I know firsthand how hard it is to push past those fears. When I started thinking about writing a book, especially a nonfiction one on the topic of personal development, I was afraid of what people would think and say. And yes, some people responded with raised eyebrows. When I started a network marketing/direct sales business in something far removed from the career I had just left, I saw similar looks of disbelief. (I still get asked if I'm making any money yet.) That's okay. It's not their dream; it's mine.

And sometimes your rewards come to you in forms other than a traditional paycheck. Vera Wang designed her own wedding gown. Look where that took her!

But who cares about all those naysayers really? If they don't want to be around you anymore, they are not your people. You're better off without them in your life.

As the great jazz saxophonist Charlie Parker said, "Music is your own experience, your thoughts, your wisdom. If you don't live it, it won't come out your horn." Yes, Charlie, I agree. And it's the same with your dreams. They are based on your own experiences, your thoughts, your wisdom. You owe it to yourself to pursue and live them. Let them come out your "horn."

But to get to a point where you can do that—and while you're at it, kick that fear to the curb—you have to truly understand and accept who you are at the core. You want to be mindful of the baggage you've accumulated and are now carrying around with you so you can leave it behind.

Do you remember when you were young and naive? You were fearless. You dared to dream, to try something new. You weren't afraid to fail. That word just wasn't in your vocabulary. That's how I felt the first time I rode my bicycle without training wheels and the first time I thought I could beat my younger brother on the tennis court. (I don't even think I got to swing the racket; I was too busy protecting myself.)

Reconnect with your inner child as you go through this process. In fact, that's your first journal exercise at the end of this chapter. Tap into that fearlessness. Because I'm here to tell you that you are still allowed to dream. In fact, you should. Just like you did when you were a kid.

Our dreams are still a part of us, but as we move through life's experiences, the baggage we pick up causes those dreams to fade. Because we're technically older and wiser, we've often traded in our dreams for more "grown-up" pursuits that leave us unfulfilled. Or we've listened to others who urged us to settle into a more realistic, responsible lifestyle. If you've done that, you've bought into their limiting beliefs, not yours.

But you're in the right place, because you're here to rekindle that flame of desire, to kick all your fears to the side and sprint to this chapter's finish line and your next chapter's starting gate. Along the way, you're going to focus on the positive instead of the list of negatives you've collected, worry less about what others think, and stop agonizing when they judge you.

Because it's a new day, and you're starting a new chapter. It's your life and you deserve the absolute best. It will take some time and a lot of self-reflection, but it is critical if you are going to design the life of your dreams. You have to understand where the fear originates, what happened in your past, and why you're still holding on to that untruth about yourself. (That's some of the baggage I'm talking about.)

Then you have to learn how to forgive and how to let it go. Only then will you be able to free up the space your mind needs for your inner truth to shine through, guide your words and actions, and keep you on the path. I guarantee that your untruths and limiting beliefs are holding you back. But I also guarantee that if you can uncover them, forgive yourself or others, and let the past go, you will be able to design the life of your dreams.

Creating it won't be all rose petals. There will be thorns. There will be dark times. But they usually happen just before the bright light and the awesomeness you find just around the corner. The dark times are just the valleys you have to go through to get to the mountaintop. Everyone has them.

So in this section, you'll start with your story. Then you'll dive into the chapters to find those messages: the things you want to take with you into your next chapter and those that no longer serve you and you want to leave behind. Finally, you'll explore the topic of dreams: why they matter, how they occur, and when they happen.

Creating a purposeful life doesn't have to be hard. Dreaming and designing your next chapter is a creative process. Be creative and intentional. Set aside your skepticism and open your mind to any strange coincidence or unconventional idea that comes your way. When it does, gently nudge the door in your mind a little farther open rather than slamming it shut. That's how you let the magic in.

Chapter 2 Exercise

What are some things you did as a child or young adult that you wouldn't consider doing now? Journal your thoughts about why you were willing to do them years ago and what's holding you back today. What could you do to reconnect with your creative, fearless inner child and rekindle your flame?

Now let's learn how to master your mind.

Chapter 3
Master Your Mind ‖

"I have a dream."

— Martin Luther King, Jr.,
American Christian minister
and civil rights activist

*M*artin Luther King, Jr., a civil rights activist with a strong belief in nonviolent protest, had a great deal of influence on American society and civil rights legislation in the 1950s and 1960s. He worked hard to bring greater equality and ensure civil rights for all people, regardless of race.

He had a dream, but he also lived it, standing among controversy and contention as a model of sound leadership, a pillar of hope, and a man of elegance and grace.

Even if you don't aspire to be a civil rights activist, you can accomplish great things in your life if you have the right mindset to make it happen. Call it a foundation. Without the right (and unwavering) mental attitude, any dream you try to design and live will crumble.

King lived his dream. He believed with all his heart and mind he could make a difference. And he made a huge impact. So you'll start there and build a foundation—a solid frame of mind—for your success as well.

The mind is an incredible, complex part of who you are. Housed inside your brain, it's a truly unique and remarkable organ that, unlike any other one in your body, has feelings and a consciousness. While you cannot see the mind like you can the brain, they work in partnership to determine how you react to situations and circumstances in your life. They also play a role in making decisions, being creative, taking initiative, and processing thoughts.

It's essential to understand how your brain works—how you're "wired"—and how you can use that knowledge to take control of your thoughts.

I never really thought about this until my major life transition. I'd heard of Sigmund Freud, the conscious and unconscious mind, and the ego, but it wasn't until I redesigned my life that I became intrigued with the power of the mind. I read personal improvement books, listened to podcasts, and watched countless videos—like a sponge.

One recurring theme piqued my interest more than anything else: if you are going to succeed at anything, you must first have the right mindset.

So I decided to try to understand this amazing, beautiful part of who we are and the role it plays in creating the right mindset. The mind is intricate and, for me, especially intriguing. Just let me say that it's not easy to wrap your head around how the brain and mind work (no pun intended).

The mind has been studied from across a variety of disciplines, some of which overlap. Neuroscience, for example, is the study of the human nervous system. Most neuroscientists focus their research on the brain and how it influences cognitive function and behavior. Psychoanalysis studies the interaction of conscious and unconscious elements in the mind and helps bring repressed fears and conflicts to the conscious mind for treatment. Psychology is the study of the mind and behavior and seeks to understand and explain how people think, act, and feel. Psychiatry is the medical specialty focused on the diagnosis, treatment, and prevention of mental, emotional, and behavioral disorders.

Now I'm no expert on any of these topics, but I wanted to share a couple of theories that helped me put my study of the mind into perspective.

The first, which is basically the concept of the left and right sides or hemispheres of the brain, comes from neuroscience. The left—the more logical, analytical, and rational side—works on known principles. Anything unknown is perceived as wrong and possibly dangerous which leads to...well, fear.

For example, every time I see a snake slithering anywhere near me, I panic. I've been known to do the "snake dance" to the amusement of my hiking companions. While I've never been bitten (and probably never even been close), I know poisonous snakes live nearby. The snake slithering in front of me is an unknown threat and therefore potentially dangerous. Fear kicks in every time. And voilà—snake dance.

The same thought process occurs when you're contemplating changes in your professional life, especially if it means you'll be pursuing something new or different. The fear of the unknown or of failure will kick in and, before you know it, your left hemisphere will logically tell you to stay right where you are, safe and comfy (if not running from the snake or doing the dance).

The right hemisphere is often referred to as the artist's side of the brain. It is more subjective, creative, intuitive, and random. Even if you think you don't have a creative bone in your body—you can't carry a tune or everything you draw looks like a stick figure—that doesn't mean you're not creative. When you took that side road to avoid traffic, you were being innovative. When you added a little something extra to spice up a recipe, you were being imaginative.

You don't have to be a musician or an author to be considered gifted. So even if you're more the analytical type, know that you can tap into this side of the brain when necessary. Because, in fact, you already do.

Neuroscience shows that the two hemispheres are interconnected and constantly communicating. That's good news because this means the whole brain is involved in processing information regardless of how analytical or artistic the task might be. And you'll need to be firing on all cylinders, so I'm going to get you more comfortable using that creative side.

I have an activity that might help you clear out some of that negative chatter going on in the back of your mind and tap into that creative part of your brain. You must do this to make room for creativity. I promise—it's just waiting for you to find it.

This exercise comes from Julia Cameron's book *The Artist's Way*. Every morning, grab a journal or a few sheets of paper and, before you allow the outside world in or let your ego try to schedule your day, write down your thoughts, whatever comes to mind. It could be worries, grandiose plans, dreams you had the previous night, or specific tasks you need to tackle that day. Even if you have nothing to say, you can just write, "I have nothing to write about today." Just keep going until you've filled three pages.

Don't cheat yourself out of exercising your creative mind. There is no wrong way to do your morning pages. You're simply getting down the stuff that rolls around in your subconscious and gets in your way of being creative. These thoughts are the impetus of doubt and criticism.

You see, your inner critic lives in the left hemisphere of your brain, the logical side. Left unchecked, it will shower you with limiting beliefs and negative thoughts, often disguised as the truth. You'll assume that those thoughts are true. You'll stay stuck and won't be able to thrive on this journey.

Your morning pages help you get unstuck.

You might be wondering why these have to be written out first thing in the morning by hand or why you need to write three pages instead of two or four. Writing your thoughts down with pencil or pen and paper takes more time to keep up with your thoughts. You don't have time to erase and edit, which means you end up with original, unfiltered thoughts.

And three pages of random thoughts is what it takes to push your inner critic aside and allow your creative side, without any pressure, to reveal itself in the words you write. (Remember, your logical side works on known principles—its truth—and tells you that unknown or original thoughts are wrong and dangerous.)

By doing this every morning, you'll eventually start to see patterns where your inner critic is holding you back, convincing you that certain known things are the absolute, only truth. But Cameron says, "The pages lead us out of despair and into undreamed-of solutions." These morning pages help you get unstuck.

Another study of the mind I find so fascinating is psychoanalysis and the concept of the conscious and unconscious mind introduced by Sigmund Freud, the famous Austrian psychologist. Interestingly enough, Freud studied neuroscience long before he introduced the ideas that now help us understand how we process information. Rather than the science of how neurons in the brain function, psychoanalysis is based on the empirical, verifiable by observation and experience.

According to Freud, the mind has two areas: the conscious and the unconscious. Outside the field of psychoanalysis, the term *unconscious* is often used interchangeably with *subconscious*. There appears to be no shortage of articles and opinions on which word is appropriate to use, so for purposes of this book, I'll use the terms conscious and subconscious.

Your conscious mind is about you—your body and how you are feeling. It is subjective in nature. Your feelings can be triggered by such things as sensations, perceptions, memories, emotions, new ideas, and fantasies. When an emotion is triggered by some external event, for example, your conscious mind feels the emotion and then tells you to think about it. It's the reason we have the fight-or-flight response in threatening situations, why we want to do more of those things that make us feel really good, and why we have a difficult time entertaining (let alone embracing) uncomfortable thoughts or situations.

In 2005, I was on a path to early retirement. My plan was to close my consulting business and ease into retirement with my husband. Then the financial crisis hit, which triggered uncertainty, anxiety, and fear. The economic situation could have been an opportunity to pivot, but instead of seeing the situation as an opportunity, I let emotion—fear—drive my decisions. As a result, I followed the path of least resistance.

Your words create feelings—even words you say to yourself—and then thoughts take over to deal with them. Your thoughts motivate you to take action, to do things that either make you feel good or avoid things that will make you feel bad. If you are doing (or even considering doing) something that might trigger emotions of fear, doubt, or worry, your conscious mind will be in overdrive telling you to fight it or avoid it.

My conscious mind was definitely in charge in 2008, convincing me I needed the financial security that only a corporate job could provide. My fear had me fleeing back to a corporate life that, while comfortable, was one I no longer desired.

The conscious mind is also where we gather information. It can learn by reading a book or listening to a podcast. It is a center of creativity—our goals, desires, and dreams come from it—and is open to new things. It's a critical player in helping us define our futures.

We are usually more aware of the conscious mind because that's where we process all the information we're bombarded with every minute of every day. It's where we judge ourselves and others, obsess, criticize, commit to losing that last five pounds, try to remember if we shut off the stove before we left the house, or decide what we're going to have for dinner. It's where we figure things out.

So your conscious mind is in the present, the now, but the subconscious mind is where all the behind-the-scenes action takes place. It's the library of information you started gathering from the day you were born. It's also the place where the actions you take based on autopilot, intuition, and instincts reside. The subconscious library contains all your memories and past experiences, including those you've repressed because of trauma, ones that have simply been forgotten, and those that are no longer important.

The subconscious has also filed away everything we've been taught to believe from Day One, whether or not we believe it to be true today. This part of the mind doesn't filter the information coming to the library; it just dutifully stores it on the shelves for future reference. Once it's filed away, the conscious mind isn't aware of it. In fact, we're usually oblivious to this library of details and beliefs that runs our lives until our conscious minds reach in to check out knowledge needed to manage a particular situation happening in the present moment.

In 2008, my conscious mind was retrieving information related to financial security (or the perceived lack thereof), opportunities for employment, marketable skills, and predictions for economic recovery.

But here's the problem: Unlike the analytical conscious mind, the subconscious mind is a storyteller. And its stories are not always grounded in the truth. The subconscious mind doesn't analyze or figure things out. It simply pieces together this unfiltered information, which includes our perceptions and beliefs regardless of when they were filed or how we got them.

I believed a corporate job was my best option. (Maybe it was the easiest path because it was familiar.) My perception was that having my own business was risky and a corporate job was the better (or perhaps easier) solution. It was a story my subconscious was telling me, and rather than allowing my conscious mind to explore options, I opted for what was familiar and safe.

The subconscious anticipates what might happen based on these memories and past experiences and fills in any gaps when necessary. This is fascinating, because the subconscious is really running the show with regard to what you believe. And it isn't always based on your current beliefs; it may fill in the blanks with any information you filed away years ago, maybe even details you've tried to forget.

Freud also believed that the things the conscious mind wanted hidden from the light of day were repressed in the unconscious and, more importantly, that things hidden from our awareness exerted the greatest influence over our personalities and behaviors.

I don't know about you, but I find that a bit unsettling. My fear of not being able to pay the mortgage or our investments not recovering had a great deal of influence. It didn't come close to the anxiety my parents undoubtedly felt when they had to put my brothers to bed with sugar water in their bottles because they couldn't afford milk. But my mind made it seem just as grim.

The subconscious is also where your ego resides. It's one of three Freudian personality concepts—the id, the ego, and the superego—that make up our complex human behaviors.

The **id**, the only personality component present from birth, includes the instinctive and primitive behaviors. It's how you're "hardwired." It's also where instant gratification resides and is not affected by reality, logic, or the everyday world.

The id is regulated by the **ego**, which receives information from the outside world including all those emotions, beliefs, memories, visual images, and experiences. The ego analyzes and stores the information, creating an internal model of how the world—your world—works. It's learning from experience.

The **superego** is your sense of right and wrong, your morals and ideals based on your past experiences, and also what society and culture declare the norm.

The ego's role is to create a balance among the id's instant gratification, the external world, and the superego's desire for an ideal solution rather than a realistic one. It must ensure that the id's impulses and the superego's idealism can be expressed in a manner that is acceptable in the real world. The mediator thinks it is protecting you so you won't be criticized or stand out.

So all this chatter is going on incessantly in your subconscious mind, your inner self. Behind the scenes, your ego is defining your reality, your world, and the way in which the conscious mind deals with present circumstances.

But your ego is not necessarily grounded in reality, and your stories may have been concocted by an "egocentric storyteller." So if you're getting the idea that what you believe may not be entirely true, you're right on. Your untruths and limiting beliefs hang out in these stories. The ego is your social mask, which thrives on approval and wants to be in control. It will fight with every available resource to keep you safe and comfortable because it operates on a fear of the unknown. That feeling of being afraid is real, but the actual fear is concocted, because you can't predict the future and you have no idea whether that scary thing is really going to happen.

Now you might be saying, "Okay, Christine. I understand the neuroscience and the basis of psychoanalysis, but what does all that have to do with mindset?"

Glad you asked.

Your mind has thousands of thoughts a day. About 95% of those occur in the subconscious, where your ego and that vast library of your past experiences reside, and where the subconscious is busy directing decisions, actions, emotions, and behaviors. The other 5% of them occur in your conscious mind, which is where you gather all that information in order to imagine possibilities for the future.

Imagination is critical in dreaming, but the trick is to be sure the ego isn't running the show. You want to make sure you're in sync with your authentic self. That you're overcoming your fear of the unknown, letting go of the false and limiting beliefs that make up the ego's reality, and acting on things you need rather than what you want.

Yes, I said *need* rather than *want*. Because let's face it—not everyone can win a million dollars in the lottery or own a house in Italy, regardless of how much they may want it.

So be aware of the power of your thoughts, because you must have your conscious and subconscious minds working in alignment if you want to live without limitations. To design and live the life of your dreams, you need to have them working together as a team, because desire (consciousness) is what gets you started and habit (subconsciousness) is what keeps you going.

You also must be aware of what the inner critic that lives in the left hemisphere of your brain is telling you so you can sort out what is true from what is just fear of the unknown.

If you don't identify and deal with those limiting or suppressed beliefs and the untruths of your past, your ego and inner critic will continue to weave those stories in a way that will sabotage your dreams.

You must understand what your particular limiting beliefs are so you can recognize the ones that aren't serving you any longer and leave them behind in your current chapter.

A **limiting belief** is something you believe to be true—about yourself, about others, or about the world—that holds you back in some way. You may believe you're not good enough, you're too old or too young, or you don't have the skills necessary to try something new. You might be afraid to try because others will judge or you might fail. These keep you in your comfort zone, planted in fear and blind to opportunities in your path and the magic that lies outside of it. These beliefs keep you stuck, often focusing on the negative. They typically show up as fear of failure, worry about what others might think, feeling you are too old (or too young), fear that you don't have what it takes, or feeling you're not good enough.

For example, my high school had a career day where sophomores and juniors were introduced to different professions and job opportunities. In my sophomore year, representatives of one of the major airlines came to discuss careers in the airline industry. I fell in love with the idea of being a stewardess. (Yes, that's what they were called then. Now they are flight attendants.) I imagined flying all over the world and seeing all kinds of exotic places. I would have signed up that day, but I didn't qualify because I was four inches too short of the 5'6" height requirement.

I thought my life was over because I couldn't be a flight attendant. Although my height was perfectly normal for a girl my age, I carried that "too short" stigma—an untruth—around for years. I convinced myself that I was too short to do all I wanted in my life.

But that's bullcrap. I'm just a little closer to the ground. Now I use it to my advantage. Can't reach that top shelf in the grocery store? I find a tall person and ask them to help. In fact, I've met the most interesting people that way. And if I really wanted to be a flight attendant, I could have applied when the airlines relaxed that height restriction. I didn't. What does that tell you?

So you can see just how silly these untruths can be but also, if left unchecked, how devastating they can be. These crazy limiting beliefs have no place in your effort to dream, design, and live your next, best chapter. If I had dwelled on the fact that I couldn't pursue my dream that sophomore year, I wouldn't have had the amazing career I did.

Another of my limiting beliefs centered around my education. I always felt a little inadequate in my senior-level executive job because I didn't have a degree (or more than one). However, I accomplished more in my career than many with advanced degrees did. And when I finally did pursue my degree, I was able to apply that real world experience in the classroom. I left my corporate job after an extremely successful career and a month after walking the stage to accept my long-awaited undergraduate diploma.

I believe that God has a plan for us. That He'll reveal it when the time is right; it's on His time, not yours or mine. You may believe in some other higher power (or not), and that's okay. My point is when you're facing one of those fabricated false beliefs about yourself, it's hard to remember that there are other factors at play.

By uncovering your limiting beliefs and seeing them for what they are, you'll have no limits to your potential. If you're staying in a job because you don't think you have any options or you think that's the only way you can make money, those are stories you've told yourself (or that you've allowed others to tell you) that aren't true.

Replace them with empowering beliefs and you'll begin to lean in to your awesomeness. And if you have to dig deep into your subconscious to identify the false truths about yourself that you've repressed for years, do it. Understand what happened to make you feel that way. Then forgive yourself, forgive others, love yourself, and move on.

So kick out the negative thoughts, all that garbage you tell yourself that isn't true and all those things that keep you up at night worrying. Instead, embrace the experience and the change. Think of it as an exciting journey. Instead of saying, "It can't be done," ask, "Why not?"

Keep an open mind, try new things, take chances, make mistakes, and get comfortable being uncomfortable, because I can assure you it will be. And be sure to watch out for your ego, because I can guarantee it will throw a tantrum when you start to think about the possibilities.

Step outside that comfort zone. Replace your fear with faith. I promise there will be magic if you do.

Chapter 3 Exercise

1. What false truths have you told yourself? Why do you feel that way? Write them down in your journal.
2. Reflect on how these may have had a positive or negative impact on your life.
3. Identify at least three limiting beliefs you currently have that may be holding you back from living the life of your dreams.
4. Write down your commitment to release the negative false truths starting today.

Okay, you with the positive mindset, let's get to work.

Chapter 4
Know Your Story

*E*very human being is on a transformational journey. And that journey is a story. Since this book is about designing a next chapter in your corporate or professional life, I'm going to focus on that. When it comes time for you to capture your story as it relates to your day job, you'll know where to start. Trust me.

I grew up in a working class family in Pennsylvania. My mother and father were wonderful Christians who worked hard, laughed often, and loved deeply. They had integrity, strong work ethics, and heart. They were honest, kind, and giving. We didn't have fancy cars or a lavish house, but we had home-cooked meals, quality family time, and sometimes the luxury of an extra bathroom (depending on the house we were living in at the time). I was the oldest of five children and my sister, the baby, was eight years younger. My sister and I were the bookends for my three brothers.

Neither of my parents had a traditional 9:00 am to 5:00 pm (or longer) office job. My mother was a nurse's aide for many years, working the midnight shift while we were asleep. My father had a route with a towel supply company that required him to get up crazy early in the morning and get on the road regardless of the weather or other circumstances. Years later, he was a well-respected, successful insurance salesman at a time when they didn't always have a good reputation. He still had long hours on the road every day, just with a different purpose and more on his own terms.

Being on this schedule is hard, especially the midnight shift. I don't know how my mother did it all those years. These hours can be extremely difficult on a person's health and personal (as well as family) life. Mom only got about five hours of sleep during the day, between fixing meals and taking care of five children, a husband, a mother-in-law who lived with us for years, and usually a couple of basset hounds and a cat. Whew! She was just short of amazing and darn close to being an angel on Earth.

When my younger sister started school, my mother decided to follow a dream that ended up being a new chapter in her life. What a trendsetter! When the local vocational school announced a brand-new licensed practical nursing program, she signed up for the first class. That was in 1969.

During that year, she worked the midnight shift, came home, made breakfast for us, sent us off to school, and hit the books. Then she would sleep for a couple of hours before getting up to fix dinner and eat with the family. She did that because family time was so central to her. Once the dishes were washed, dried, and put away (no dishwasher back then), she would study for a while, try to sleep a couple more hours, then get ready for her next shift.

The entire year was like that. Lather. Rinse. Repeat. And she did it without complaining or regrets. She must have been exhausted! Or she drank an awful lot of coffee.

But she was following her dream and that's what mattered most. When she graduated, we all stood proudly alongside her. I'll never forget that moment. For years after that, she took required continuing education classes. All while still working the midnight shift and caring for her family.

Your past is part of your story, and my parents are most definitely a huge part of mine. They instilled in me values of integrity, honesty, trustworthiness, determination, and hard work. All of that influenced a part of my story that didn't unfold until years later. And it played out better than I ever could have expected. Isn't it funny how that happens?

You see, my parents were highly intelligent people who chose to enter the workforce after high school instead of pursuing college degrees. (Well, my father served in the military right out of high school before landing a job. He also tried out for the baseball minor league but wasn't selected. I wonder how things would have been different if he had been.) But the point is, higher education wasn't part of their aspirations. Making a living and raising a family was integral. And because I loved them and the life they had created so much (and it was really all I knew), I believed I should follow their lead.

I convinced myself that getting a job instead of heading off to college was the right thing to do. It became a false belief later on and a mask I wore for an awfully long time. On the outside, I wanted everyone to know it was okay to follow what society deemed appropriate. Go to school, get a job as soon as you can, and stay in that job until you retire. On the inside, I knew there had to be more.

So I chose what some might call "the simple life." And don't get me wrong. There's nothing wrong with that. In fact, some might say we could gain a lot from getting back to the basics and to what matters most.

At the age of 16, I landed a job as a receptionist at a local real estate office. It was one of those partnerships with the local high school, intended to give students experience in the work-force. At the time, our high school offered three tracks of study: business, academics (college preparation), and technical/voca-tional, which focused on practical knowledge so students were able to find a job in the trades after graduating. I was in the business track, and my receptionist position solidified my path into the workforce rather than pursuing any higher education.

Now mind you, I'm not being critical of any of these paths. It takes all kinds of skills and talent to maintain our vibrant economy. We need skilled, dedicated workers with advanced degrees in the sciences, engineering, and medical professions. I certainly want someone who has completed medical school and has the credentials to prove it treating me! And I feel more confident crossing a bridge that has been designed by a civil engineer. We desperately need young people with interests in the technical and vocational paths that result in skillsets needed for our specialized trades. And we also need various kinds of support staff to make sure organizations run effectively.

In my case, I'm just saying that I had perhaps taken the path of least resistance, and the more I looked around me, the more I thought maybe it hadn't been the best decision.

But back to my story. I graduated at the top of my class and truly loved the world of academics. But I didn't know what I wanted to do with my life. I had no idea how I would pay for college even if I wanted to attend. The thought of asking my parents for money was definitely out of the question. I took the easy way out. So my storyteller, my subconscious mind, told me that I wasn't college material, I didn't have the money, and I wouldn't be able to make it on my own.

We become so deeply wrapped up in these limiting beliefs like they're our life support that we can't even begin to see the possibilities that surround us.

I told myself that not going to college was okay. But deep in my core, I knew it wasn't. That was a mask I wore for years.

The first chapter in my story about life in the corporate world was landing my first job after high school. My next chapters included a job in the financial world, my career in the electric utility industry, and my role as an entrepreneur. Along with my experiences growing up, those all defined who I am today. Each chapter since then has been different. Some were by design and others by default. Along the way, I added and accomplished some of my dreams and goals.

Your story changes and evolves, and as you move from one chapter to the next, it's important to learn from your experiences. I am grateful for each and every one, however painful or pleasurable it was at the time.

That's how you learn from the messages in each chapter, even if it was messy or unpleasant. (*Especially* if it was messy or unpleasant.) Your messages may have been similar to some of these:

- Avoid jumping to conclusions.
- Be grateful for what you have.
- Trust yourself.
- Be courageous.
- Take risks.
- Embrace the unknown.

You have a choice: You can either focus on the mess and let all that negative energy control your emotions and life, or you can learn from it. Focusing on the mess doesn't change the fact that certain events happened that caused it. You can't change the past. But what you can do is reflect on those circumstances that contributed to your mess and figure out how to not let history repeat itself. That's learning from your mistakes, because when you know what went wrong and you know how you could have done better, you won't repeat them. You'll do better.

As you reflect on each chapter, practice gratitude. Nothing will get you through the tough times like recognizing what has gone right in your life and appreciating what you have. By practicing this regularly, your attention will be directed toward the positive aspects of your life instead of the negative.

Grateful people are able to recover more quickly from setbacks or stressful situations. As a result, they are less likely to let harmful events pull them into a downward spiral and more likely to grow in difficult times. Think about how we, as a society and as a human race, come together during difficult times like 9/11, Superstorm Sandy, Hurricane Katrina, tornadoes, economic crises, deadly wildfires, and worldwide pandemics.

When we're creative and flexible and we come from a place of love and compassion, we show just how resilient we are as a human population.

Being grateful for what you have also makes you more resilient. And resilience helps reduce stress and improves mental, emotional, and physical health. Think about how your past might have been different had you practiced gratitude for what was going right at the time.

Above all else, recognize that you have the ability to change. You always had that capability; you probably just didn't act on it. Recognize what was going on in each phase of your life, and be aware of the stories you told yourself (or you've allowed others to tell you) in earlier chapters, because they may be at the root of the negative or limiting beliefs you have about yourself now.

These limiting beliefs are not facts. They weren't then and they aren't now. None of them need to be true. You are just allowing your subconscious storyteller to convince you otherwise. So once you identify them, you can rewrite your story the way you wish it to be.

While you're at it, get rid of the masks. It took me a while, but I finally decided to ditch the "okay to not have a degree" mask. My dream to earn a degree from The Pennsylvania State University spanned about 40 years. It had to be Penn State, end of story. I grew up in Pennsylvania and the university was (and is) a huge part of the culture. As an avid college football fan, there was no other choice but to be among those who proudly declared, "We are...Penn State!" Walking the graduation stage at the age of 62 was an amazing experience.

Also, check the habits you formed in each chapter or carried along the way. Your behavior can either help propel you into a new phase or sabotage your efforts in ways that keep you firmly in that safe, comfortable place you long to break out of but can't seem to.

As Zach Galifianakis said in the movie *Due Date,* "You better check yourself before you wreck yourself." Don't wreck yourself.

So look those habits that are no longer serving you straight in the eye (you might need a mirror for this) and start to create new ones that will better serve you in the future. Acknowledge and deal with the ones you don't want before they have a chance to ruin the chapter you desire before you even have an opportunity to design it, let alone live it.

As you move from one chapter to the next, think about what you learned from your experiences, the times you failed, and the times you succeeded.

Then feel grateful for what you learned. Recognize you have the ability to change. Check your habits. Then gather up all the messages you find in your mess and ditch the ones that no longer serve you. They are just baggage. Finally, note all the good ones and carry them forward.

Even better, recognize when your mess is really your message. Then go out and share it with others.

You are not alone in your pursuit of the perfect day job. Unless you're independently wealthy, you need some type of work or career to support your lifestyle and provide for your family. Share those experiences and messages: the trials, heartaches, and success stories. It's your opportunity to lift someone else up. Encourage them to make adjustments in their story, their journey, to make this thing called life so much easier.

Isn't that what it's all about? That's the reason I decided to write this book, to share my story and experiences. As you've read, I was flung abruptly into my latest chapter, and my transition was far from graceful. But I learned a lot, and now the message I'm sharing is how to skillfully and graciously manage any mess that comes your way and come out in a much better place.

With a lot of reflection deep into my core, my soul, I discovered how much my family and friends had influenced my life and how that guidance—along with the experiences and messages I received—contributed to the strong, confident woman I am today. It all matters.

And now, sharing my story may be what you need to hear, to give you the confidence you need to know that your story matters, that *you* matter.

Your story is what makes you unique. Don't let anyone tell you otherwise.

Chapter 4 Exercise

Write your story. This way, you can leave what no longer serves you in the past where it belongs, change your routines, and begin to create new habits so you can move forward. Start by answering these questions.

1. How did the people and events influence your professional and personal life?

2. What limiting beliefs and masks are sabotaging your plans for the future?

3. Write down the behaviors and habits that are sabotaging your plans for the future (EX: Netflix binging or having an extra glass or two of wine every night). Do these truly make life better or are they just false beliefs?

In the next chapter, you'll break your story down into chapters, uncover what you liked and disliked about each period, and turn them around so you can write an awesome new story that will have you leaping out of bed every day.

Chapter 5
Analyze Your Chapters ‖‖

"In the middle of a difficulty lies opportunity."

—Albert Einstein,
theoretical physicist

*J*ust a side note before we continue: The focus of this book is on designing a new chapter in your professional life or career. It is not necessarily about your personal life, although some of the mindset work you do may overflow into your personal dreams and aspirations. That's perfectly okay.

The reason I say this is because in my experience, it is difficult to completely separate the two. My career *was* my life, for better or for worse. When I had a particularly stressful day at work, I could almost count on that stressed-out mindset following me home like a thundercloud over my head. Even after a half-hour commute, I just couldn't let it go.

You're going to work on that. Letting things go is essential for staying in the right mindset for success.

As I share my story with you, think about how your past work experiences can be formed into chapters in your story. Later, I'll be asking you to think about them, what you were good at, what

45

you didn't like, where you struggled, and how what you were doing made you *feel*.

So let's begin.

Life In The Financial World

As I mentioned earlier, my first professional chapter began with a work-study program in partnership with a local business and my high school. Note that some of my chapters and choices were a product of the philosophy at the time, what was expected, and what was available to students and workers.

When I attended, students were prepared for one of three paths. Later, the system put greater emphasis on entering college right out of high school rather than train for a trade or immediately enter the workforce. The school system was designed to match labor environments, and that was usually eight hours a day in some form of structured setting.

During high school, I worked at a local real estate office where I performed the following tasks:

- Answered telephones
- Interacted with customers
- Honed my shorthand and typing skills
- Learned how to effectively solve problems
- Handled cash, including balancing funds at the end of the day

After graduation, I worked for a savings and loan association and a couple of credit unions. The savings and loan hired me as a teller, so I was handling and balancing cash and posting payments to accounts. I was also interacting with employees, customers, and the general public.

All three financial institutions provided on-the-job training, which included telephone etiquette, customer service skills, handling complaints, problem solving, data entry and, of course, robbery and burglary protection. (Thankfully, I was never robbed!)

After a few months at the savings and loan, I applied for and was awarded a position as a mortgage loan processor. Loan processors were required to know and understand lending requirements and regulations, how to request and analyze credit reports, and how to evaluate applicants and applications for credit-worthiness. I learned as much as I could, and I found the process fascinating.

But my world was about to change. My fiancé landed a job on the west coast. When I moved across the country and started looking for employment, the knowledge and experience I gained at the savings and loan served me well. Within weeks, I had a teller position with the local credit union. All the customer service and banking skills, knowledge, and experience were easily transferrable. I liked the work and was good at it.

After a few months, my husband was transferred to a town about 60 miles away. I knew there was a different credit union in my new town, but quite honestly, I was getting a little tired of applying for jobs and then leaving after only a couple of years. I was interested in having a career.

When I resigned, the credit union manager just smiled. "My friend manages the credit union in that town. Let me give him a call and see if he has an opening. Would that be okay with you?"

Inside I was screaming, *OKAY? Of course it's okay!* But what came out was, "Sure," thinking it was a long shot that there would be an opening. As it turned out, both managers were interested in adding mortgages to their loan program portfolios. They had been exploring options and looking for just the right person with the experience and knowledge to lead the effort.

His friend didn't have an opening, but he created a position for me. The regulations and processes for securing a mortgage are more complex than they are for buying a car or getting a personal unsecured loan. My experience blazed the trail; I was uniquely qualified. I loved the challenge of putting that knowledge to work in building something from scratch.

Soon I was managing the entire loan department, mortgages and installment loans, while conducting training and overseeing other activities. My customer service and problem-solving skills were often put to the test when dealing with difficult customers and collecting on delinquent accounts.

One customer never balanced his checking account and became irate when he was overdrawn. Always convinced it was the credit union's error, he would march into the lobby with checkbook in hand, face beet red with rage. Everyone would scatter...except me. I found it rewarding to calm him down, help him figure out the problem, and fix it. He always thanked me.

Another customer was a long-haul trucker. I have a great deal of respect for people transporting the goods and products we use every day across the country and back. But this particular customer always seemed to fall on hard times. His payments were frequently late for various reasons. New tires (seemed like he needed them every month). New engine parts. A person or company not paying him on time. You name it, there was an excuse for it.

One day, he came in to make a payment on his loan. Instead of showing me the money, he dropped a huge, fresh salmon on my desk. It's a little hard to put that in the teller's drawer and balance it out at the end of the day. Plus we weren't allowed to accept gratuities. Even a beautiful and most certainly delicious fish like that. I thanked him for the kind offer, explained why I couldn't accept it, and extended the deadline for his payment. He thanked me.

One customer turned in his car the day he entered the witness protection program. We felt like we were in the movies and that at any minute the car in the parking lot was going to blow up. Honestly, I couldn't possibly make this stuff up.

I loved this position. The on-the-job training opportunities were amazing. I loved interacting with customers and employees, solving problems, and using my knowledge and skills to design new programs. What I didn't like about this chapter were collections (they were emotional and stressful), the limited opportunity for advancement, and a regulatory structure that left little room for creativity.

My next chapter actually came looking for me.

Life In The Electric Utility/ Hydropower Industry

So there I was, sitting at my desk working on loans in various stages. I looked up and saw one of my customers coming my way. He sat down and put two job descriptions on my desk.

"These are two brand-new supervisory positions that were just announced at the local public utility district," he said. "Positions like these are rare, and this organization is the best one in the county to work for. I think you'd be an excellent choice and you should apply."

I thought, *Why not? I have nothing to lose. I have a job I like, so if I don't get either of these new positions, I'm not out anything.*

I applied and got an interview. Since competition was stiff, I interviewed a second time before being offered the customer service supervisor position. I was ecstatic!

That was the beginning of my 30-plus-year career in the electric utility industry, and where my passion for the energy industry and hydropower began.

During my first few years at the utility, I supervised various departments, including customer service, credit and collections, conservation, and customer billing. What I had learned in my financial chapter served me well in this one. The regulations and policies were similar in some areas, such as the process of collecting money and balancing work at the end of the day.

The credit and collections processes were also very similar, with one major difference. With financial institutions, loans typically have collateral (such as automobiles, boats, or houses) that can be repossessed or foreclosed on. But with electric utilities, no collateral exists. The electricity has already been used and cannot be returned.

The only recourse is to follow a process to collect the amount owed, and if you're unsuccessful, the last resort is to disconnect their power. Disconnecting an essential service is way worse than repossessing a vehicle. The job of a collector at an electric utility is difficult work, mentally and emotionally.

One exciting challenge was learning the billing process. This included scheduling and supervising meter readers who spent their days in the field instead of an office, ensuring bills were accurately produced and mailed according to the schedule, and identifying and resolving billing discrepancies and abnormalities.

Energy conservation was a totally new concept for me. Oftentimes, I assisted customers who had high bill concerns. (In fact, I still use these analytical skills to help friends, neighbors, and people venting on social media to find the "culprit" in their home that is consuming more electricity than it should and causing their bill to be higher than it needs to be.)

Can you spot the common threads?

- Communicating and interacting with people effectively
- Exploring options and finding solutions in a variety of circumstances and situations

- Building and maintaining good relationships with employees, customers, and the general public
- Applying effective listening skills to better understand issues and come up with solutions
- Learning and improving

These weren't skills traditionally taught in the classroom, but the on-the-job experience prepared me to advance to a manager position. From there, I became the first female director at our company, which is the equivalent of a vice president in private corporations.

After a few years at the utility company, I gravitated toward more government and public affairs work. I recognized the challenges on the horizon as our country began to wrestle with reaching balanced, sustainable solutions to complex issues regarding energy and natural resources.

Our company was a major player in this multi-purpose river system, a development that spans four states and dates back to the conservation movement of the early 1900s. The hydropower system was designed as the economic workhorse for the entire region, but it became much more than that. It is now a critical component in the region's healthy economy, greatly enhancing the lives and lifestyles of its people.

Low-cost electricity allows farms to irrigate and businesses to prosper. Barging enables low-carbon, efficient transportation. Water management protects cities, homes, and people from flooding and allows for recreation. Emissions-free generation keeps the skies and environment clean. The system (through electricity rates) also provides the infrastructure, programs, and funding for fish and wildlife.

But societies and major industries evolve with advances in technology and new scientific knowledge. History is often forgotten. In the adaptive process, customs, norms, and beliefs are challenged, and conflicts occur. Politics and people in general become strident and polarized. Emotions cloud facts. Hydropower (similar to agriculture, manufacturing, and the timber industry) was extremely misunderstood and mired in controversy.

Societal issues are complex. My role as a government affairs professional was to present the historical prospective, the current situation, and possible solutions for the future. I had the distinct pleasure (or distinct displeasure) to witness what goes on behind the scenes in politics and in particular what happens in the halls of Congress and state legislatures.

It was often exasperating. Sometimes, I had to bite my tongue. Other times, I couldn't wait to get away from it so I could scream about the absurdity of it all. But after 20 years of debate (and endless litigation), the region was no closer to a solution. I was burned out and stressed out, and I felt like I had stayed long after my expiration date. My elevated blood pressure, panic attacks, and lack of energy were evidence that my emotional and physical health had suffered the consequences.

Still, I was a passionate senior-level manager with an essential role that I took very seriously. This career taught me to be open-minded, to seek facts and sort through emotions so I could craft the best possible solutions that were sustainable for generations to come. Above all else, this experience showed me how to be kind and treat others with respect even if we had to agree to disagree.

Once again, I was learning skills that weren't taught in the classroom but are so critical in navigating professional and personal circumstances that occur in the corporate world. Compensation is a great example.

While compensation plans aren't commensurate with societal issues, they are a motivator in an organization's effectiveness. Employees understand that jobs and responsibilities carry different weight within an organization. They don't expect everyone within the company to be paid exactly the same, but they do expect compensation to be fair, reasonable, and supported by research and data.

I was the only female director in a highly technical world that was at the time traditionally dominated by men. Once you reached director level, you were no longer a front-line engineer sitting at a drawing table or at a computer using programs to design your utility systems. You were no longer a lineman. Instead, you managed those employees and the work they performed. So you had to know something about the work, but you were expected to take a much broader view and steer the organization as a whole.

This structure put the directors on a more equitable scale, because the organization valued their ability to manage projects and people as well as the day-to-day activities, while also anticipating how the organization might need to pivot to ensure its future success.

Because directors were compensated more on interpersonal than technical skills, one would think they would be evaluated accordingly. That wasn't the case. In reality, the directors were still evaluated based on experience and knowledge in the technical arena, placing a higher value on engineers, accountants, and others with technical degrees (the men) and a lower value on communication and customer service skills (the lone woman...me).

So I gathered all my stellar performance appraisals and presented my case to the general manager, seeking clarification on what I perceived as unfair and discriminatory treatment. While he had the authority to manage employees and administer the compensation plan according to an adopted budget and personnel policies, he was required to seek support from the governing board to raise any salaries above the mid-range for his directors.

The board had supported above mid-range salaries for all of them...except me.

I later learned that one of the board members had said that I "didn't really need the money because my husband had a good job with benefits. And I was making a lot of money for a woman."

I had hit the glass ceiling and it was real.

But wait—it gets better.

This board member had also said that I should be "home in the kitchen," which was hilarious because I can barely turn on the stove and my husband is darn close to a gourmet chef.

But his comment was ridiculous also because by this point organizations should have been actively working to change the discriminatory policies and practices that had been the societal norm for decades. In fact, a report issued by the Glass Ceiling Commission in 1995 noted that only about 5% of senior management positions were filled by women. The women who did hold senior positions (typically in areas not considered traditional pathways to executive positions, such as human resources and public relations) were compensated less than their male peers.

While that has changed over the years, the number of senior management positions filled by women is still less than 30%, with women human resource directors lagging male counterparts by 20%.

As I saw it, I had several options. I could stay in an organization that expected me to continue to perform with excellence but didn't value my worth or my stellar performance and grow bitter in the process. I could sue for discrimination. I could find another job. Or I could learn to cook so I could stay home in the kitchen. (I'm kidding, of course.)

Should I really stay in an organization that I'd lost confidence in, like some other "walking wounded" I had actually tried to counsel? I knew I was meant for more. I didn't want to feel trapped. I wanted a career I was passionate about, one I truly believed in. My heart told me to move on.

Could I find an equivalent job in a small town? I would have to completely switch careers or seek a position with a commute of more than an hour each way.

Litigation wasn't my first choice, but I did seek legal counsel. The attorney was incredibly wise. He told me, "I would like nothing more than to sue this organization, and you have a strong case."

I started to smile, but it quickly faded as he proceeded to give me a big dose of advice and a lesson in reality.

"No one wins in a lawsuit. And the case could take years and drag you and your family through all kinds of mud in the process."

I knew he was right. I didn't want the emotional stress.

"But you are a smart, talented woman and you don't need them. If there are no options in town, why don't you put your skills, knowledge, and talent to work in another way by consulting?"

Why hadn't I thought of that? I knew other successful consultants in the same industry. Some were dear friends. But I hadn't considered it for myself because I was afraid I wasn't as qualified, wouldn't be as successful, and might even fail. I was scared of the unknown.

Recognize a pattern? Yep, those limiting beliefs were worming their way into my life again.

It was time to assess my life. The opportunities for personal and professional growth in this chapter were remarkable. Through my involvement in trade associations and as a key figure in public/government affairs work for the utility on the local, regional, and national levels, I had gained a wealth of industry knowledge and expertise. There was opportunity for advancement. I was passionate about the industry and my work.

What I didn't like were the politics, polarization, and negativity that engulfed the industry issues, and my personal feelings and disenchantment with the organization's internal politics. I took a look at the good and bad in this chapter, and realized that my knowledge, expertise, and passion for the industry was still a driving force in my professional goals. To let go of what was no longer serving me (the glass ceiling and feeling undervalued as an employee in particular), I decided to leave my corporate life and consult. And that started my next chapter.

I left respectfully, even though in the end we had agreed to disagree.

The Life Of An Entrepreneur

As I turned a spare bedroom into my new office, I reflected on my decision and steps forward. Yes I was afraid, but I was also determined. Sipping my coffee and sorting through emails without interruptions felt good! I thought *I could get used to this.*

Zbeau, my 125-pound Bouvier des Flandres was my office mate. (The herding breed originated in the Flandres region, which encompassed areas of northern France, Belgium, and the Netherlands centuries ago. *Beau,* French for handsome, was so common that we added a *Z* for variety.) Zbeau loved having me home all day. His presence made life interesting. Especially when he would walk on the papers I had organized in piles on the floor, or when he let out a loud groan or snore at an inopportune time during a conference call. He was the best office mate!

Ah, the life of an entrepreneur.

I started with one small contract, but once word got around that I was freelancing, the referrals started coming.

The work was invigorating. I loved working on the same hydropower and natural resource issues with the bonus of being able to work on my own terms. I could work with people and organizations I wanted to work with, on a laptop while sitting in the afternoon sun in my courtyard, taking phone calls while out walking with Zbeau during the day—my definition of heaven. I loved everything about life as an entrepreneur, especially the flexibility, time freedom, and life on my own terms.

I had stepped outside my comfort zone, and I was starting to see and experience the magic.

A little over a year into my new chapter, I learned that an attempt to take control of the generating assets owned and operated by the organization I'd called home for 15 years was forthcoming. It was the first license competition known to the industry. The effort was well-funded, and was a serious matter. I was invited to meet with the team leading the effort. And when I did, word quickly got back to my former employer. (I can only hope the first person to hear about it was the man who had said I should be home in the kitchen.)

My former general manager had put together a team of experts to fight the effort, and one position wasn't filled. That person would lead and coordinate the public and government affairs work. He said I would fill that empty position, and gave a directive to make it happen.

"Come back as an employee," the negotiator proposed.

I declined, not wanting to do that again. But I did offer my services as a contractor, drafting a multi-year contract with terms and conditions that would protect me in the most certain event that I would have to sign a noncompete agreement.

Before signing the contract, I asked my attorney to review it. "I think I missed an opportunity to hire you as a negotiator," he said with a twinkle in his eye. I felt vindicated!

After the contract was signed, I went to work. But this time, it was on my own terms. I had a wonderful life as an entrepreneur with an income that was based on my worth instead of outdated discriminatory policies. Over the next four years, the team developed and implemented strategies that ultimately helped them set the company's direction for the next four decades.

Eventually, my contract ended and I prepared to move into my next chapter. By this time, I had moved to another state and intended to phase out my clients and move into retirement at a young age. Sadly, that wasn't in the cards.

I was still enjoying life as an entrepreneur and I had some amazing clients with interesting projects. One of them was the local electric cooperative. The story of how I landed that particular contract makes me smile even today. We had just moved into our new home when we received the cooperative's annual meeting packet. Since much of my career had been in the electric utility world, I eagerly pored through all the information. (I know. I'm an energy geek.) After reading the general manager's message to the members, I told my husband I had to respond. Two days later, my phone rang.

The GM's administrative assistant will take all the credit for me being hired, as well she should. She had read my letter and told him it was obvious that I knew the industry. He called and invited me to lunch, where he asked me to come to work for him. But I wasn't willing to give up my life as an entrepreneur, and I didn't want to work full-time for anyone else. I was determined to live life on my terms and retire at a young age.

We settled on a part-time contract arrangement. I got to work on some communications and relationship issues. It was challenging and exciting, even though it was quite intense at times. I loved collaborating with the general manager, the employees, and the members to solve problems, develop strategies, write, and communicate.

But I was right back under the thick clouds of negativity and controversy. Now it was like a double whammy. It wasn't just negative, polarizing politics about energy resources; the cooperative was split on some major issues and decisions that had been made at the local level as well.

(On a more positive note, I will say that I have been blessed to work for and alongside three brilliant general managers over the course of my career in this industry. Each had a different management style, but I learned a lot from each one of them, and I am grateful for the knowledge they shared and the support they gave me at the time.)

Learning doesn't always have to happen in the classroom. I'm a living, breathing example of that.

When the economy crashed in 2008, my retirement plans crashed along with it. I found myself entering a next chapter that was much different from what I had planned or expected.

The cooperative had hired a new general manager in the midst of their turmoil, and he presented an opportunity. Essentially, the door to what I had known for years had reopened and I walked right back in to a senior-level position. Part of the agreement moving forward was that I would phase out my clients, close my business as an entrepreneur, and totally commit to my new position. I was back in the corporate life I'd said I never wanted again.

I knew what that meant: the loss of freedom and flexibility, once again setting the alarm clock each day, trading my home office for a half-hour commute, and being part of a corporate world that was still dominated by men.

But as I carefully considered the financial market and our personal finances, it seemed logical to opt for a more stable income and a generous benefits package. I told the general manager I would give him one year. Being in public/government affairs and in communications was stressful enough. I really didn't want or need the additional stress that came with being a woman in the corporate world.

After nine years at the cooperative, I finally left corporate life once and for all.

I really can't complain. I'm truly grateful for the opportunity to work alongside smart, talented, and positive people (for the most part).

During that time, I was able to work on some amazing projects, write a history book and articles for a monthly publication, design a new process for developing and implementing the organization's strategic plan, and organize a grassroots effort. My work was recognized by various industry and trade associations on local, state, and national levels. I also had the opportunity to mentor others and I loved it. I very much appreciated the support I had received in my career and loved being able to pay it forward. It is extremely rewarding to help someone build their self-esteem or gain the confidence to tackle, and succeed at, a new responsibility.

What I didn't like about this chapter was the daily commute, loss of freedom and flexibility, the negative politics and polarization, and corporate life in general.

But being a mentor spilled over into my personal life as well when I decided to finally finish the remaining classes required for my degree. I found myself in online classes with students of all ages and from all walks of life. I was perhaps one of the oldest students at Penn State's World Campus (their online program), but I didn't even know there was an energy-related degree until 2012. By then I was nearing the end of my corporate career.

In 2017, Penn State featured an article about my higher education journey that had spanned 40 years. In that article, I told them that I loved learning and often regretted my decision to enter the workforce without pursuing a degree at the university when I had the opportunity.

My pursuit of a degree was a little different because it was happening alongside the advancement of my career. Since the Energy and Sustainability Policy degree program tied closely to my career experience, I had the opportunity to share my expertise and knowledge of the industry as well as my perspectives on the complex energy policy issues that the world continues to grapple with today.

Attending commencement and walking the stage to accept my diploma with all the other graduates was bittersweet. I knew I would miss the intellectual part of interacting with other students and the instructors, but I also knew I had done my part to bring real-world experience into the world of academics. It was my hope that this would improve the quality of future energy conversations, debates, and policies. And if I was also successful in creating intrigue and possibly recruiting some of the next generation of industry professionals, I had definitely contributed.

Ultimately, I think a degree prepares you for and enhances your work or career, regardless of when you obtain it. But a diploma alone doesn't make you passionate about that career. And even if you have a degree in one field, it's okay to pivot if you're not happy doing what you're doing. Your talent, education, and knowledge can be applied elsewhere. You and the world will be better off as a result. I know brilliant attorneys who are no longer practicing law and are instead using their talent to live their dreams and change the world in way more positive ways.

So I graduated with a BA in Energy and Sustainability Policy and left my corporate gig for the final time the following month. Who says you're too old to pursue your dreams? Don't you dare believe it. I'm living proof that you can. And if I can do it, you can too. I was proud and honored to be part of the degree program at that particular time. And I don't think it was by mistake that I got my degree later in life. I believe it was an example of divine timing or said another way, "When it's meant to be, it will be."

And that started the chapter I'm in now.

Life After Corporate

I'd like to tell you that I designed this chapter right from the start. But that would not be true. Had that been the case, however, I probably wouldn't be writing this book.

I wanted to do something, but I wasn't sure what. I considered consulting for the energy industry, but to be honest, I was burned out. It was time for me to pursue something more positive and let others take up the charge where I left off. After all, that's what I had worked so hard to do: develop, encourage, and support people who had the talent, interest, and passion for the industry and pass the baton.

A year or so earlier, I had been introduced to the world of network marketing/direct sales, and I found the idea of generating residual income through a home-based business intriguing. I could sell products that had been life-changing for so many people and build my own team. That meant I could surround myself with positive women and men and again have the opportunity to coach them to success (whatever that meant to them).

Quite honestly, I wish I had found the world of direct sales during the 2008 Great Recession when the economic crisis was destroying corporate life as we knew it. The dynamic women I have met who bet on themselves, pushed past their fears, tapped into their creativity, and connected with their authentic selves didn't play it safe. They pivoted, left their corporate jobs for new opportunities, and are crushing their personal and financial goals today.

But sometimes life just gets in the way. And this chapter of my life didn't start out anywhere near what I thought it would be.

Two months after I left my corporate job, a wildfire broke out, rapidly spread, and raged out of control just two miles from our home. It gave me a whole new appreciation for people who have been threatened and harmed by natural disasters. The sheriff posted mandatory evacuation orders on our gate, which we found on our evening walk. We panicked, running around the house throwing valuables into the two vehicles. After discussing the situation with neighbors who were monitoring the fire's progress (they had a view for miles), we opted to stay in our home.

The next morning, I decided to examine and organize what we had pitched into the vehicles the night before. Among the family heirlooms, artwork, clothing, dog food, medications, and valuable paperwork, I found a bag with two cans of tuna and two cans of diced tomatoes. I reminded my husband that if we did have to evacuate, we'd be going to a town that had grocery stores and restaurants.

For the next five weeks, firefighter crews roamed the neighborhood, assessed the property for defensibility, and marked each home accordingly. Law enforcement and the National Guard set up checkpoints to safeguard the area. Even though we were on mandatory evacuation, which meant we might have to leave without official warning, we never did. The whole experience was surreal to say the least.

Then we sold my dream home and moved in with family for 10 months until we found our next one. While it was a very special time, it was also very unsettling. My library of books and my pantry were in boxes piled up like a barricade in my home office. I was constantly looking for the one that had the extra jar of Dijon or can of chicken soup.

After we found a house, I focused on overseeing the renovations. Two weeks before we were to move in, we had a freak snowstorm and I had to scramble to find someone to clear the driveway so they could finish the renovations in time for the moving company to deliver. Around the same time, one of my beloved Bouvier des Flandres, Jacmel, was diagnosed with an aggressive cancer, and we lost him at the young age of seven. My female, Kaya was almost 13, so it was just a matter of time for her. The move had been extremely difficult for both females in our household.

I didn't handle the beginning of that chapter very well. I had lost my sense of purpose and passion for life. I was depressed, lacked focus, and cried a lot. The strong, confident woman who had for years stared back at me from the mirror was nowhere to be found.

Sometimes you just have to pick yourself up. Because only you can control how you react to the situation you're in.

I'm finally back on track. It took a lot of mindset work, meditation, and business coaching to gain the clarity I needed to truly start living life by design instead of default.

Now that you've heard my story (at least, the chapters in my professional life), it's your turn to document your own so you can analyze it in the same way. I've told you this part of my story so you know that you have choices. You don't have to stay stuck or in a position that doesn't value your worth. You can put your interests and talent to work to follow your dreams and be passionate about what you do.

You deserve more and you are meant for more.

Chapter 5 Exercise

Use whatever creative tool you desire: the companion journal, a notebook, piece of paper, or your computer or phone.

1. Think about what you liked about each of your work experiences and what you were good at. Contemplate what would make you sprint out of bed some mornings.

2. Then consider what you didn't like and where you struggled. What made you want to hit the snooze button and throw the covers over your head some days?

In the next chapter, you're going to discover your truth—who you really are and what makes you tick.

Chapter 6
Uncover Your Truth ‖

*I*n this chapter, you're going to dive into the specifics of your unique skills, interests, and talents and how they make you *feel* so you can get clear on what will serve you well in your next chapter and what no longer serves you or will get in your way.

Make a commitment right now to let go of any beliefs, perceptions, and emotions that don't align with your truth as it unfolds in this process. Up to now, your ego has had you believe many things about yourself that aren't necessarily true so you stay trapped in that mindset. You're too old or too young, don't have the necessary skills. You're foolish to try. You'll fail. The best way to quiet your ego is to make a conscious decision to find your truth—the good, the bad, and the ugly. That means staring some memories in the face then letting some of them go.

In this process, you're also going to lose your false self: that feeling of not knowing who you are anymore. You're going to stop letting your ego help you decide, because that's just living by default. The "fabricated you" shows up when you dread getting out of bed, you feel a weight on your shoulders as you're getting ready to go to work, or you find yourself just going through the motions.

No one should go through life just waiting for each workday to end. You deserve more and you are meant for more.

And don't worry. You have everything you need to do this within you right now. To identify what doesn't align with your true self and let it go. To recognize your unique gifts. To live in alignment with your truth and your purpose. You don't have to go back to the classroom to figure it out.

So let me start by asking you this: Who are you without limitations? Take a deep breath and really ponder this. By doing the exercises up to this point, you've already started to formulate your dream, one that doesn't include any of your false truths or limiting beliefs. It should include the activities you are so passionate about that you get lost in them, losing all track of time. That's you without limitations.

Still a little unsure? You've already started the work when you identified your likes and dislikes in the last chapter. I'll show you how it came together for me.

The work I enjoyed most nurtured my creative spirit. My medium of choice was (and still is) writing. I've dabbled in art and I play the piano (rather poorly), but I've always loved to write.

Creative writing is considered entertainment, while technical writing is viewed as education and information. Each serves a different purpose, but the creative process is rooted in both. Writing in the corporate world is more technical in nature, and some wouldn't call it creative at all. I beg to differ. Writing testimony, magazine articles, press releases, website content, a history book, or just about any other communication for public consumption needs your creative mind at its finest if you're going to make it interesting, informative, factual, and understandable.

Technical writing is typically more concise and precise but, like creative writing, it can also be (and in some cases should be) informal and friendly, especially since the point of the document is to get others to understand the idea you want to convey. Writing a technical document from the creative perspective takes skill and talent.

I received numerous awards for my written material, including one from the Council of Rural Electric Communicators and National Rural Electric Cooperative Association for *Follow The Line: A story of Coos-Curry Electric Cooperative, Inc. and how one man's vision and determination changed lives and lifestyles.* Still, my ego told me I would never make it as a writer outside the corporate world.

By now, you recognize that was a limiting belief. It was not part of my truth. I knew I had talent and wanted to write in my next chapter. The first thing I needed to do was quiet my feelings of doubt and fear, ditch the limiting beliefs that told me I couldn't do it or wouldn't be any good. Then I needed to make a decision and act on it.

So here's what I said: "I can and I will. Watch me!"

You, on the other hand, may have a burning desire to break into the field of technical writing. If so, I've got good news for you. According to the US Bureau of Labor Statistics, the demand for technical writers is projected to grow 8% from 2018 to 2028, due to the continued demand for instruction manuals and the ability to communicate information in the scientific, medical, and technical fields. That means opportunities for you to write for an organization or as a freelancer.

You may have aspirations to complete your degree, learn a new language or instrument, become a gourmet chef, take acting lessons, or start your own business.

You can and you will. We'll watch you.

In my next chapter, I wanted to inspire others. I valued my role as teacher, coach, and mentor in my corporate life, and I wanted to continue to influence and enhance the lives of others. That's one reason I entered the world of network marketing/direct sales and why I also coach women to gain the confidence and clarity they need to design their next chapters based on the concepts I'm sharing with you in this book. I was still interested in being associated with people, but not as part of an organization run by someone else. These options allowed me to create my own community.

And the limiting belief that I won't succeed? Ditched that one too.

So what were some activities I disliked and intended to leave behind? Politics, having to work with negative people, being on someone else's schedule, a daily commute, and trading time for money come to mind.

Consulting in that industry no longer served me. It didn't make me feel good. And since feelings are indicators of your personal reality, it wasn't my reality anymore. As my sister would say, "Let it go." So I did.

But leaving behind this world I had been so passionate about, where I was known and respected and where I could write to my heart's content, meant doing something different. And that's where a whole host of limiting beliefs reared their ugly heads.

- What if I can't find a new passion?
- What if I can't make it as a creative writer?
- What if the economy crashes again?
- What if it takes a long time to find work?
- What if my next job is even more stressful?
- What if it takes a long time to find work?
- I'm too old.
- I'm afraid.

The list goes on and on.

To get to your truth, you have to face these limiting beliefs and rewrite them to align with your true self. For example, I used to say, "Although I enjoy writing, I can't make a living doing it unless I'm in the corporate world." That is a limiting belief that I rewrote to say, "I will ensure that writing is a key component of my work and I will tackle it fearlessly."

So I just started writing. I posted inspirational quotes and thoughts on social media and learned I wasn't alone. Others in transitions or facing uncertain times longed for inspiration, and they thanked me for my positive thoughts. When we got a new puppy, I started posting her experiences (written from her perspective) on social media. Within a couple of days, she had quite a following with hundreds of likes and comments. And now if I don't post for a week, I hear about it.

Then I started blogging and I got the same great feedback. And that happened because I kicked those limiting beliefs and ego to the curb and pivoted. People said I was a talented writer. I was inspiring. They wanted more. They wanted a book. So here it is. Maybe next I'll write a children's book based on my puppy's experiences.

Because now I know I can do it and I will do it. Watch me.

If you have a strong desire to do something—if it's YOU without limitations—and you still think you can't do it for some reason, think again. If you have the right mindset and the right character, you absolutely can.

So now it's time to get to your truth. The exercise at the end of this chapter will help you find the limiting beliefs that are holding you back. Once you identify them, you'll rewrite them so they are in alignment with your truth. You won't be able to design your perfect next chapter if you let them hang around.

Chapter 6 Exercise

1. Who are you without limitations?
2. What have you always wanted to do, keeping in mind your likes and your unique skills and talent? Why do you feel that way?

3. What don't you like about your current professional life, and what no longer serves you? Why do you feel this way?

4. Pick at least one limiting belief you have and rewrite that to align with your true self.

Now that you've uncovered your truth, turn the page and see where that might take you.

Chapter 7
Find Your Zone Of Genius ‖‖‖

*B*efore you start to figure out where your true interests lie and what you might like to focus on in your next chapter, you need to consider your values—the core beliefs that guide your behavior. They are your personal code of conduct, characteristic traits you believe are an integral part of your personal and professional life.

When you determine your guiding principles, life decisions become much easier. For example, say you're trying to decide whether to take a new position where you'll need to work 50 or 60 hours every week and travel a lot. If you place a high value on spending time with your family, that's clearly not your best option. You'll say, "Pass" before you make the mistake of signing away your family time and living with regret. If you think politicians are evil and you're considering a job as a legislative aide, it's probably not a good fit. But if you love helping your parents at tax time and an opportunity to help senior citizens opens up at the local H&R Block, you might pursue it.

Values will also help you through difficult times or even a full-blown crisis. When the shit hits the fan, staying true to your core beliefs will keep you focused rather than stuck in panic and survival mode. When they are clear, they act as a guide and a steadying hand, keeping you on track. When you're clear on them, you're more likely to act in ways that serve your highest good. When

73

you're living in alignment with your values, you feel more positive about yourself, the decisions you make, and your life in general.

Your values are a part of you, whether you've articulated them or not, and they may evolve over time. If you are working 60 hours a week with little emotional or physical energy left for your family, you're most likely stressed out and frustrated. What may have worked before you had a family no longer serves you, so now it's time for a change. When you know your values and can pivot when events in your life change, you will be able to make decisions quickly and easily. In this case, you'll start looking for work that provides the balance you're looking for and, when opportunity comes your way, you'll be absolutely sure about the decisions you make.

So how do you uncover those core beliefs that are truly important to you? One way is to reflect on events that have happened in your life (personal and professional) and consider the underlying character trait that may have caused the reaction, feeling, or emotion. Maybe a coworker violated a policy or code of ethics. What if I had accepted that beautiful salmon as payment instead of actual money for that guy's 18-wheeler? If one of your values is integrity, you will most likely have little tolerance for others who are unethical or dishonest or who don't follow the rules. And you certainly wouldn't want to spend time in a work environment where you are surrounded by them!

A cool trick to get to the root of it is to use an action verb instead of writing it down as a noun. For example, the word *integrity* may mean different things to different people. But when you say "always do the right thing," you've made the definition crystal clear.

One of my standards is to be an inspiration to others. In my current life chapter, I have found new and exciting ways to inspire others to live their best lives because I designed it that way. Another is to live my life with passion and purpose. To weave that into my new chapter meant digging into my likes, dislikes, and strengths. Once I had a clear idea of what would help me live a more positive life, I focused on that and left the negative behind. See how this all fits together?

I'm also at my best when I am balanced and grounded in my truth. Being grounded means believing I'm good enough, having confidence in my abilities, knowing I'll be fine no matter what happens, and pursuing a meaningful, purposeful direction for my life.

Now think about some of your negative memorable experiences. What happened? Which of your values may have been violated?

I treasure having meaningful relationships. In our fast-paced world, we sometimes forget to pause and spend time with those we love: our families, friends, and even our pets. Nurturing those relationships is vital, but I haven't always done my best. Now that my parents are gone, I wish I had spent more time visiting them (even though we lived on different coasts). And I regret the times I felt I was too busy to go for a walk on the beach with family members (human or canine). I'd love to rewrite all that history.

But you can't rewrite history, can you? You can, however, stay true to your core beliefs so you have no regrets.

Chapter 7 Exercise A

Uncover Your Values

1. Think about one or two positive memorable experiences that recently occurred in your work life. What was going on around you? What values might you have been honoring at the time?

2. Now think about what core beliefs represent your character. What characteristics in others best align with and resonate with your standards of behavior?

Now pull out the work you did to get to your truth (from Chapter 6). You're going to use all this information to get clarity on the options for your next chapter using a tool I developed called the Zone of Genius.

Chapter 7 Exercise B

The Zone of Genius matrix is designed to help you identify your ideal career path based on your personality traits, values, and interests. Each quadrant addresses the unique ways your core beliefs and career interests intersect. Knowing the characteristics of the ideal relationship between the two means you can design a career path that is fulfilling, energizing, and inspiring.

Before you determine your Zone of Genius, read on to learn a little more about each one. You might circle or highlight terms that best describe your interests or talent.

The **Creator** is a visionary, an entrepreneur. This type likes to color outside the lines. The Creator is an independent thinker who is passionate, motivated, innovative, creative, and resourceful in achieving goals. Through their entrepreneurial spirit, a Creator turns passion into a career or business opportunity built on their own terms. Entrepreneurs who love what they do and are extremely dedicated to the businesses they create are in this category. They are confident, flexible, and decisive and seize every opportunity to get the job done with a high degree of excellence. Creators include people in these roles:

- Artists
- Consultants
- Freelance writers
- Inventors
- Network marketing professionals
- Small business owners

A **Leader** thrives on collaboration and a strong team environment to get the job done. Often working within an organization, Leaders are coaches, facilitators, and connectors. They understand the organization's business model and strategic initiatives, and leverage team strengths to accomplish the organization's goals. Leaders are trusted advisors, effective communicators, and problem-solvers. They are patient, empathetic, and supportive. Leaders are typically in these roles:

- Grassroots organizers
- Human resource professionals
- Managers
- Organizational development specialists
- Tribe/community builders

The **Mastermind** has a specific area of expertise and may have invested significant time in obtaining a license to engage in a particular business, occupation, or activity. The Mastermind is skilled and knowledgeable and loves their chosen field, desires a stable work environment, is confident and competent in providing technical expertise, and is often structured and analytical. Often thriving in a structured organizational setting, Masterminds are in jobs such as these:

- Architects
- Computer systems analysts
- Engineers
- Health care professionals
- Information technology specialists

The **Champion** desires work flexibility, a strong work/life balance, and a stable income to support their lifestyle. They are excellent in support roles, thrive in a team environment, value personal growth, avoid risk, and are patient, intrinsically motivated, and energetic. A Champion often has a side interest (such as music, art, or photography), but unlike the Creator, believes that turning that passion into a career would take all the fun out of it. Champions (usually as part of a team) are often in these types of roles:

- Chefs
- Event coordinators
- Social media managers
- Tax advisors
- Website developers

CREATOR	LEADER
[Visionary/Entrepreneur]	*[Team Builder/Collaborator]*
Adventurous	Coach/facilitator
Desires life on own terms	Communicator
Flexible	Connector
Innovative	Empathetic
Motivated	Patient
Optimistic	Planner
Passionate	Problem-solver
Path-forger	Process-oriented
Resourceful	Trusted advisor
MASTERMIND	**CHAMPION**
[Provides Professional Services]	*[Supporter]*
	Avoids risk
Analytical	Desires work flexibility
Desires stable work environment	Excellent in support roles
	Intrinsically motivated
Licensed	Patient
Loves chosen professional field	Strong work/life balance
	Values personal growth
Structured	
Technical skills	

Find Your Genius

Now it's your turn to find your Zone of Genius. You know you're unhappy at your job but feel lost about what to do next. These questions will help you think about your perfect workday, identify what motivates you, gain clarity on your ideal career path based on your values and interests, and help you figure out which zone you align with most closely.

It's the first step in uncovering what drives and motivates you so you can dream, design, and live your next, best chapter.

1. In my ideal job I...
   a. Work for myself doing something that I love, regardless of pay.
   b. Have something that keeps me on my toes, trying new things.
   c. Have a secure position with attainable goals and good pay.
   d. Show off my expertise.
   e. Do something meaningful, contribute to the big picture.

2. My friends and family describe me as...
   a. Nurturing, giving, and helpful.
   b. Creative, spontaneous, and unique.
   c. Smart, ambitious, and no-nonsense.
   d. Social, the center of attention, and friendly.

3. In school, I...
   a. Struggled to stay focused.
   b. Participated in school plays.
   c. Got straight A's.
   d. Tutored others in my free time.
   e. Was part of lots of clubs and teams.

4. My worst fear is...

    a. Being stuck in a boring desk job.

    b. Having no control over my life and future.

    c. Not knowing how to do my job.

    d. Feeling helpless.

    e. Not getting recognition.

5. In my current job, I feel...

    a. I'd like to quit and start my own company so I can be the CEO of me.

    b. I'm not given enough responsibility and leadership.

    c. The glass ceiling is alive and well.

    d. Uninspired.

    e. I need a better work/life balance.

6. I want to...

    a. Do my own thing.

    b. Lead other people.

    c. Discover something new.

    d. Be happier in my current career path.

7. If I went back to school, I would...

    a. Take classes that would help me start my own business.

    b. Try something totally different.

    c. Learn leadership and management skills.

    d. Take classes to enhance my current profession.

    e. Study something that's more fun and interesting.

Scoring

If you consistently answered A or B, you're in the **Creator** zone. **Leaders** normally pick B or C, **Masterminds** select C or D, and if you had mostly D or E responses, that would resonate with **Champions**.

So where did you land—Creator, Leader, Mastermind, or Champion? There's no right or wrong answer.

As for me, I'm a Creator. I love the lifestyle and the creative mindset of an entrepreneur, especially if I can bleed over into the Leader quadrant in order to fulfill my passion to coach, mentor, and help others succeed. I'm ambitious and resourceful, and I love working for myself, hate being in a boring job, crave meaningful work, and want to be inspired and inspire others.

It's common for your genius to spill over into other quadrants. Does yours? If so, how? Remember you can always find ways to add in some of the skills, talent, and interests from the other quadrants as you start to design your new future.

You've taken the time to uncover the real you. Now it's time to be true to yourself. You will have characteristics and talent in more than one area. But you will find one path that rises to the top.

In the next chapter, you're going to tap into your dreams.

Chapter 8 ‖
Envision Your Dream

"A dream is the seed of possibility
planted in the soul of a human
being, which calls him to
pursue a unique path to the
realization of his purpose."

— Sharon Hull,
executive coach

*D*reaming is critical when you are designing a new
chapter that fuels your passion and purpose in life.

I'm not referring to the dreams you have while sleeping. Let's leave that up to psychoanalysts like Sigmund Freud who have devoted their lives to researching, interpreting, and analyzing those dreams we have while we're asleep.

I'm talking about your waking dreams—your life goals or your purpose. When you affirm your true goals and desires, the Universe will mirror and expand on it. In fact, you should expect and trust that the Universe will support your dream once you've affirmed it.

You may not be accustomed to thinking that God's will for us and our dreams can coincide, but they can.

"For I know the plans I have for you," declares the Lord. "Plans to prosper you and not to harm you, plans to give you hope and a future."

— Jeremiah 29:11

Whether or not you believe in God or some higher power, isn't that what we all desire?

But you see many of us, especially those in the baby boomer generation, thought that financial stability and job security were first and foremost in the race to success, which usually meant landing a job right out of high school or college and staying put until retirement. Unless we knew exactly what we wanted to do for the rest of our life and landed that dream job on Day One, we really didn't think about our dreams.

And if they revealed themselves later in life when we were comfortable and secure in our job? Fuggetaboutit. By then you were probably hanging around the water cooler telling everyone you were living the dream while all the while you were just walking dead on the zombie path to retirement.

How many times have you heard someone say, "Just living the dream" with all the excitement of a robot. Chances are on the inside they're really screaming, "I wish I were doing something—anything—else with my life!"

What a waste of a life. If this is you, my heartfelt desire is that you will be inspired to change that.

What if you dared to dream and take action?

Some have. One that stands out for me is the 31-year-old welfare mom turned billionaire in 14 short years. J. K. Rowling's story is a fascinating one. She wanted to be a writer from an early age. That was her passion, her dream. At six years old, she wrote her first book; at age eleven, she wrote her first novel.

She obtained an undergraduate degree in French from the University of Exeter then worked as a researcher and bilingual secretary in London for Amnesty International. During this time, her idea for a story of a young boy attending a school of wizardry, *Harry Potter,* was born. Seven years later, and with only three chapters written, Rowling was jobless. She felt like a failure yet continued to write.

Two years later, the first book in the series was accepted by a publisher, after having been rejected by 12 other publishing companies. Her editor told her to get a day job since she had "little chance of making money in children's books." Yet she continued to write.

Soon after, she received a grant that allowed her to keep writing. And the rest, they say, is history. In 2004, *Forbes* named Rowling as the first person to become a US-dollar billionaire by writing books. This allowed her to join the ranks of entertainers such as Steven Spielberg, George Lucas, and Oprah Winfrey. And this was when Hollywood was still only halfway through the eight *Harry Potter* films, well before the launch of her other artistic endeavors.

She had a dream and she followed it with passion. With a degree in French. The Universe not only said, "Okay," but also expanded on it. What if she hadn't even asked or tried? What if she had used her unrelated degree as an excuse?

There's tremendous power in being passionate about your dreams. You may not want to write or have aspirations to be the next J. K. Rowling or Oprah, but your dreams are just as important, just as worthy.

What would you do if you could do anything, without limitations? What is your big, lofty goal?

Turning a dream into reality takes some effort. But don't shy away from it, because unless you bring it to the forefront, a dream will only remain a desire in the subconscious mind.

Dreams will help guide your way to finding the passion and purpose in the life that you crave. Along the way, your desire to achieve them will make the journey exciting. You'll bring about a new enthusiasm for life. You'll be on a path of your own design and will have taken full control of your life.

One word of caution: Be sure you're not chasing meaning-less goals, ones that don't light the fire deep down inside you. The ones that don't feed or nurture your soul. This includes goals others said you should pursue. If you're staying in a job because the money is good but you dread going to work every day, the money alone isn't worth it. You're drowning out what really matters.

If you're staying in a career because you (or someone else) invested so much in your education, but you can't stand another minute in your cubicle, you're wasting your precious life. If you feel obligated to assume responsibility for the family restaurant when you really want to start your own, you're chasing someone else's dream.

Just go for what you want—but be sure you know *why* you want it and how it will make you *feel* when you get it. Make sure you let your heart in on it too. In fact, start with your heart. Because if realizing your dream won't make you feel joy—and you know that in your heart—why waste your time on it?

You might be wondering why so many people don't follow their dreams. I wondered that myself, and I believe there are many reasons.

Some people have had their dreams knocked right out of them. Maybe they feel they aren't talented enough or smart enough. Someone may have told them not to do that "thing." Perhaps they tried once and failed. If this is you, I hope the exercises you've done in this book will help you find the courage to try again. After all, these are your dreams to pursue. Don't let any-one take that away from you. Don't give away the power you have over your own life. When J. K. Rowling's editor told her to get a day job, she looked the other way, and I'll bet she never looked back!

Aside from kids who knew at an early age they wanted to be astronauts, doctors, musicians, or artists, not many of us have ambitions when we're young that stick with us an entire lifetime. In fact, dreams can change course more than once in a lifetime and can also change the course of your entire life. They can determine your occupation and your inner desires in any chapter.

What about you? When you were little, what did you dream of becoming? Did those aspirations change with time? How closely does your current profession align with who you thought you wanted to be when you grew up? Remember, J. K. Rowling didn't seriously pursue her dream until she was in her thirties, and she did it with a degree in French.

My dreams didn't involve a fairytale ending. Aside from my interest in being a flight attendant, I really didn't have much of a vision for my life until later chapters. During my career in the electric utility industry, my dream was to be a knowledgeable, respected advisor on energy issues. And I accomplished that.

Another dream was to obtain a college degree. Not just from any university, I wanted a degree from The Pennsylvania State University. I accomplished that.

My dream now is to inspire others, help them find clarity and confidence to truly live life by design, and to help them find passion and purpose in any chapter in life. I have created an amazing community that positions me to influence the lives of women in transition. I serve these women by taking them on a transformational journey using the written and spoken word, by sharing my stories, my experiences, my lessons, and all the knowledge I've gathered in my own transition. I am unstoppable and unwavering in my desire to encourage and inspire them to believe that they were meant for more and can absolutely design their life to achieve it.

So don't settle for what's familiar. Dreams require a person to stretch, to go beyond what's known. You can't chase a dream with gusto and stay safe in your comfort zone at the same time. It just doesn't work.

Step outside. Take risks. But be ready to pivot, because when you're trying something new, you're going to have disappointments and experiences that seem like failures. That has caused more than one person following their dreams to just give up trying. But it's those failures, those times when things don't go as planned, when you need to get up and keep going.

Don't be afraid to fail. Learn from your mistakes, keep trying, and don't ever quit. I know it's hard, but try looking at each failure or disappointment from a different perspective. Focus on the positive, and that message that will rise from the ashes of your mess.

When I left my corporate life to be a consultant—giving up a job with great pay and benefits—I felt like a failure. But every moment of defeat has a flip side, a silver lining. Mine came in the form of a contract on my terms out of a series of events I never imagined.

Remember to go easy on yourself. Accept that you can't do things perfectly no matter how hard you try. Even though they'd like you to believe it and social media says it's true, no one is perfect. Give up the need to control everything in your life. Do yourself a favor and stop thinking you have to do it all and be everything.

Be perfectly imperfect. Acknowledge and accept that you will make mistakes. Keep your sense of humor. And keep moving forward.

Once you start following your dreams, you will never lose interest in life. Your daily routines and each step on your journey will be exciting instead of boring and monotonous because you have your eye on a highly desirable prize. You'll be energized and motivated. Who doesn't want that?

Chapter 8 Exercise

Find a quiet place. Take out your journal with the exercises you've completed. Think about who you are without limitations.

1. What fuels your passion?
2. What gives you purpose in life?
3. What would make every day at work perfect?
4. If someone asked you how you were doing and you replied, "Living the dream" and you meant it, what would that look like?
5. Use words or drawings to capture it here.

It takes a lot of imagination, courage, and confidence to follow your dreams. So dream big. And remember, the journey matters as much as the result. Don't rush through it. Savor it.

In Section II you're going to put some structure to your dream and in Section III you'll be learning how to live it.

SECTION II

Design It

Chapter 9
Follow Your Path ‖

*D*id you ever read John Updike's Rabbit series? In the second book, *Rabbit Redux,* the character Harry "Rabbit" Angstrom is brought back so readers can see what's going on in his life a decade after the first book.

I've always liked that word. Redux. Since we're going to start with mindset again—bring it back, so to speak—I'll call this mindset redux.

First, a short recap.

You undoubtedly recall from Chapter 3 that mindset is a mental attitude or inclination. A fixed state of mind that is housed in the brain, a remarkable organ that, unlike any other organ in your body, has feelings and a consciousness. You learned about how the mind and brain collaborate to determine how you react to situations and circumstances in your life, even though you can't actually see the mind like you can the brain. You also learned about how the mind has been studied from many different points of view across a variety of different disciplines, and that while these various fields of study focus on different aspects of the mind and the brain, they often overlap.

You also read about the conscious and subconscious mind, limiting beliefs, and your ego. And about how you should keep an open mind, try new things, take chances, make mistakes, and get comfortable being uncomfortable if you want to pursue your dreams.

(In fact, feel free to review the first mindset section if you need to, because it's the foundation for the work you'll do moving forward.)

In this section, you'll take some key steps toward your next chapter. These stepping stones include your vision, goals, objectives, tactics, and specific actions to turn your dream into reality.

As I've said before, it all starts with mindset.

To design something means you'll be engaging the creative side of your brain. In fact, everything we do requires creative thinking and creative choices, though we seldom recognize that.

But you've got a good start on it already because you've uncovered what you like and dislike about your current job, career, or work environment. You've identified those things that are no longer serving you and determined what is causing you to hide in bed hitting the snooze button.

Now you're going to start formulating your plan for creating the perfect workday so you can enjoy earning those dollars that support your lifestyle.

Your limiting beliefs and your ego are probably in overdrive right now. They might be telling you that you're not good enough, that you can't do it, that you're too old. Or they might be trying to convince you that you have to stay on your current career path until you retire, because that's what is expected or because you don't deserve to enjoy a different lifestyle.

Yet none of that is true.

First, you must give up the idea of perfection, because no one is perfect. Instead, vow to be perfectly imperfect. You'll be much happier.

You are not too late and you're not too early. Everything happens according to divine timing, when it's supposed to. You can design your next chapter from wherever you are in your story, regardless of the career you're in or your circumstances. Just start where you are. Build the path. You can drag your ego along—high heels, hiking boots, or tennis shoes and all.

So you have a degree or a job in something that no longer serves you. So what? Take what you have learned and apply that knowledge in a new way.

You get to decide how and when to use your education. And remember, education comes in many different sizes and packages; it's not always a diploma hung on a wall (or hidden in a closet).

I consider myself a lifelong learner, and I suspect you might be the same. My higher formal education spanned four decades and didn't start until I was close to 30 years old. But I learned a lot from on-the-job training and from coaches, mentors, and coworkers along the way. I read a lot of books. I even completed a management internship program during college football season at a rival university, surrounded by a sea of red and white. (That was torture for a Penn Stater who bleeds blue and white!) If I can do that, you can do anything!

So if the career path you're designing requires new knowledge, I know you'll be excited about that.

Maybe your ego is telling you that you can't or shouldn't do this because you don't have a creative bone in your body. And you might tend to agree. But that isn't true either. Think about it this way: If you're just going through the motions and you're bored or fed up with your day job, that's just your version of lather, rinse, and repeat. That daily "ho hum" is blocking your creativity. It's your ego keeping you inside your comfort zone. Reframe those limiting beliefs and perceived roadblocks, get unstuck, and embrace what might lie ahead.

You deserve it.

Remember, you are in charge of your life, and you can design it so your conscious and subconscious minds are in sync with your inner soul. You may not know where your passion and purpose lie now, but you can certainly get some clarity on what it could be in the future. Your life will make better sense if who you are, what you believe in, and the path you are on are in perfect alignment.

If you've been writing your morning pages as I suggested, you're already recording thoughts that are rolling around your subconscious and causing you to doubt and criticize yourself. You've already started to see the ways your inner critic, that left side of the brain, is holding you back. You're starting to notice the limiting beliefs, negative head talk, and unproductive patterns and getting past that to the truth. You're thinking with your artist's brain. You're being imaginative and creative! Good for you. Keep it up. It's a new muscle that needs to be exercised regularly.

I didn't have those tools when I was thrown into my new chapter. And I didn't have the right mindset either. Digging deep into your soul to gain clarity is something I wish I had done during the uncertain economic times of 2008. I had my own business, but I was afraid of what the recession would mean to our personal finances and our lifestyle. Ten years later, I did what I should have done nine years earlier. Then again, if I had done it then, I probably wouldn't be writing this book.

So anyway, a couple of years ago, I did this. About the time I realized that I had stayed in my corporate gig way past my expiration date and I had decided to leave the utility world behind, I was introduced to a completely different business model.

Unlike some other entrepreneurs, I'm not a fly-by-the-seat-of-my-pants kind of girl. I'd had some exposure to the direct sales model. Well, sort of. I'd had friends involved with Amway, Melaleuca, J.R. Watkins, and Tupperware—all direct sales brands that go way back. Many years ago, I was a skincare and makeup consultant, although I truly became one to get the product discount and to help a friend rather than to build a business for myself.

But the direct sales industry today is noticeably different. In fact, there are now thousands of brands, including household products, essential oils, cookware, travel, virtual assistants, cosmetics—you name it. As I considered my options and started researching various brands and company structures, it became clear that if I was going to be successful, it would have to be with a product and a brand I could be passionate about.

I was introduced to a brand developed by two brilliant and world-renowned dermatologists who had developed life-changing products and set up an online business model that didn't require home parties, deliveries, or inventory. The skincare junkie in me raised her hand and shouted, "I'm in!"

I tried the anti-aging products and was totally wowed. Stress had taken a toll on my skin, and I knew I looked older than my years. My skin was dull, the dark circles under my eyes looked like the "eye black" on a football player, and the wrinkles on my face and neck were more prominent than ever.

Within just a couple of months, the gal in the mirror told me this skincare was just what I needed to get my skin—and my self-esteem—back in shape. While I had bathroom drawers devoted to the latest and greatest skincare products I had collected over the years (and they weren't cheap), they were soon cleaned out and taken to the skincare product graveyard. The retail sales clerks at major department stores who loved to see me coming would have to find someone else's bag to fill.

Now mind you, I'm in that top left quadrant of the Zone of Genius, which houses entrepreneurs and visionaries. I'm a Creator with a foot in the Leader quadrant. I saw it as my ticket to get all the benefits of being a business owner without all the headaches of the models I had known previously, without the risk associated with a brick-and-mortar small business (which I really didn't want anyway), and without trading time for money.

Plus the timing was perfect.

The Great Recession had sparked the gig economy over a decade ago. With that came the direct sales business model and freelance opportunities, as many Americans were saying goodbye to the traditional 9-to-5 lifestyle in favor of a much more flexible schedule that worked around their needs.

In 2019, nearly 57 million Americans (35% of the workforce) were freelancers and 6.8 million were direct sellers. Freelancers contributed nearly a trillion dollars to the economy, and direct sellers contributed $35.2 billion. During the economic downturn of 2020, 14 million additional workers lost jobs, significantly more than the 8.8 million left unemployed during the Great Recession.

Just think about the opportunities. Maybe you're in the right place and time too.

Let this book be the inspiration you need to let your creativity out. Because let's face it—you're not reading this because you have all the answers, are in your dream job, and have a life of more meaning and purpose than you can imagine. You are stuck. My desire is to help you get unstuck.

Start with your limiting beliefs and what you don't like then pivot to your skills and talents and tasks you enjoy. Let your imagination and creativity take control.

When I did this, I found that I had options. I explored them with an open mind and open heart. That was my pivot into a business that allowed me to surround myself with positive, energetic, smart, business-savvy women who had my back. I was finally part of a fun community, a tribe. I was able to build a team of like-minded women who desired the same entrepreneurial lifestyle. As a coach and mentor, I could help women in any chapter of life be successful on their own terms.

That was definitely creative. I was back to my life as an entrepreneur, but in a totally different business model and industry. It felt amazing.

A year or so later, when I was in the thick of my life transition, I was introduced to a brilliant business coach. She had built an extremely successful online business with another direct sales brand, and since I was in somewhat new territory, I thought I could learn a lot from her experience. I had no idea.

She listened carefully to my story about leaving corporate life, earning a degree, selling my dream home, living out of boxes for 10 months, and losing our two beloved Bouvier des Flandres. She was compassionate and understanding as I went on to tell her how lost I felt, and how I longed to regain my confidence. She was willing to coach me through building my business online, but she thought I had more to share with the world that would lead to serving people in multiple ways.

So I listened with an open heart and an open mind, from the creative side of my brain. And that's why I'm where I am today. It's all because I took a chance and asked for help. And as a result, I found someone who saw the potential in me that I was unable to see in myself.

I didn't just hire a coach; I made an investment in myself...and it paid off.

Now I'm on a mission to help other women do the same, because I know I'm not the only woman who has wanted more or felt lost, has longed to leave a profession, career, or job that is no longer serving them, or has just ditched a corporate job. Not the only woman who has struggled to define her next chapter and live with purpose by design, not default.

Chapter 9 Exercise

Right about now, your ego is likely in overdrive, telling you that you're not good enough, you can't do it, you're too old, you have to stay on this career path because that's what your degree is in, or you just don't deserve to live the life of *your* dreams.

Acknowledge it and take a step forward.

1. Write down everything holding you back.
2. Then let it go. Tear up or burn the piece of paper you wrote it on if you have to (just be careful).

If it comes up again (and it will) or if you have new self-sabotaging thoughts, do this exercise again. Then let it go. Again.

Remember the dream job you conjured up in the last section? The one based on what you would really love to do, what you're good at, what gives you joy, what you liked to do as a child? You're going to use that information in the next few chapters to help get clarity and take action.

Chapter 10 ||||
Set Your Vision

W hen you think about vision and mission statements, big corporations like Amazon, Nike, Southwest Airlines, and Apple, Inc. probably come to mind. But corporations are made up of people, and that's why it's so important for individuals to also have a clear view of where they're going and why.

In 1978, four young musicians from Dublin, Ireland, formed the rock band U2. Since then, they—as a band and as individuals—have lived their vision for a better world through their mission and core values. They vowed to improve the world through their music and influence using core beliefs of valuing people and a commitment to excellence and continuous improvement. Their thoughts and actions have addressed human rights, social justice, and matters of faith. More than just ideas packaged in song lyrics, they have created a culture. Their vision is a world that is vastly changed for the better because of their efforts: it focuses on tomorrow. Their mission is how they will do that: it focuses on today.

That's the work you'll do in this section. You'll start with your vision, which will set your course, your destination for your journey. While complementary, a vision and a mission are not interchangeable.

Your **vision** is your preferred future—who you want to be and what you want to do, and how you want things to be—usually written as if you are already there. It's your dream wrapped up in a package. Writing it is the first step; it can help put things into perspective and be a light that guides you and keeps you on your path.

Let me ask you. What would you do if you knew you couldn't fail? That's your vision.

Your **mission statement** is the foundation for most of what you'll be doing in designing your next chapter. It should be a clear, concise, inspiring, and memorable statement based on what you stand for (core values) and what you'll do today (goals and objectives) to get you to where you want to be (your vision). Having a clear mission will help you initiate, evaluate, refine, and recalibrate the actions you'll take on your journey. It will become your guide, keep you from getting distracted in a world full of distractions, and help you pivot when you need to.

Don't know where to start? That's perfectly understandable, especially if this is the first time you've ever thought about it. I've already mentioned U2. Let me give you another example, Sir Richard Branson, founder and CEO of The Virgin Group. Branson was told at an early age that due to his poor academic performance and dyslexia, he would either end up in prison or become a millionaire. What choices! He started his first business venture at the age of 16, and the rest is history.

Today, Branson's personal mission is "To have fun in [my] journey through life and learn from [my] mistakes," and as it relates to business it's to "know how to be a good leader and always try to bring out the best in people." This carries over to his corporate vision to "create a better world, where businesses are driven by a strong sense of purpose that balances their needs with those of people and the planet" and corporate mission to "use our entrepreneurial spirit and resources to disrupt and reinvent every sector we're in, helping to transform the way everyone does business along the way."

Not being afraid of failure and learning from your mistakes is critical to his success as a visionary and entrepreneur. He obviously pushes himself outside his comfort zone and he's a great example of how you can find the magic when you do. He says his secret to bouncing back "is not only to be unafraid of failures but to use them as motivational and learning tools. There's nothing wrong with making mistakes as long as you don't make the same ones over and over again."

So don't be afraid to fail.

As you contemplate your vision, be sure to dig deep and consider *why* you want to do what you've said you wanted to do. Why do you have this vision?

I know that's a tough question. But if you truly understand your why, you'll be able to stick with this whole idea of designing and living your dream. Your why will keep you in the game for the long run.

You see, every person operates on three levels: what they do, how they do it, and why they do it. We all know *what* we do: the products we sell, the services we offer, or the jobs we have. Some of us know *how* we do it: the things that we think make us different or stand out from the crowd and the processes we put in place and use. But very few of us can clearly articulate *why* we do what we do.

There are exceptions. Think about Apple Inc., a company whose why is to challenge the status quo and offer their customers simpler alternatives. Notice how the brand's why doesn't say anything about computers. It's much deeper than that. They design products based on innovation and feeling, and the result has created an almost cult-like following of loyal customers and employees.

Think about U2 again. While you might expect the band's purpose or why to be topping the charts, selling records, and making a lot of money, their actual mission (based on their values) is to improve the world through the group's music and advocacy. This commitment to people and excellence governs their individual and group decisions and actions and has created a culture like none other.

The why is the purpose, cause, or belief that drives us. It's the reason you get out of bed in the morning, the kind of drive I associate with Steve Jobs, Sir Richard Branson, and lead singer Bono. Once you understand your why, you'll be able to clearly articulate what makes you feel fulfilled and you'll have a better understanding of what drives your behavior. You'll have a point of reference for everything you do moving forward, and you'll be motivated, inspired, and intentional.

Your why should be deeply personal to you. So if you are already headed down the money road, dig deeper. Because if it's just about the money, you're only focused on a result and you won't be committed enough to stick with it. So instead think about your why in terms of what the money will do for you and how it will make you feel.

Likewise, if the reason you want to have a next chapter is about pleasing other people, you won't be committed enough. Because it's scary out there, right? Romi Neustadt perhaps said it best in her book *Get Over Your Damn Self.* "You need a bulletproof why to get you through the tough times. And that why has to be about you and for you."

Howard Schultz's why runs deep. After spending time in Italy as a new employee, Schultz returned home with a vision of building a company that treated people with dignity and respect, and coffee houses that served up experiences based on daily rituals and a sense of community in addition to coffee. His why became the foundation of the Starbucks we know today. Even though he stepped down in 2017, his why continues to drive company's vision, "to establish Starbucks as the premier purveyor of the finest coffee in the world while maintaining our uncompromising principles while we grow" and their mission, "to inspire and nurture the human spirit—one person, one cup, and one neighborhood at a time."

Make your why bulletproof. And then always base your decisions and actions on it. Trust me. You'll stand out as inspiring and authentic—a true leader.

Do you see how important it is to understand your personal vision and mission in life, and to be clear on why you want to pursue them? You must do so if you want to align yourself with just the right career. For example, if you've decided you want to start a new business, you want to make sure your core beliefs are aligned with the vision you have for that new business and that you have qualities in the Creator quadrant. If you've decided you're going to stay with your current employer (either in the same position because you love it or in some other one because you love the company), you'll want to make sure your personal values are aligned with your company's business vision and mission and also with qualities in the Mastermind or Champion quadrant.

Think about Starbucks again. The brand's guiding principles are to be the "premier purveyor of the finest coffee in the world," "inspire and nurture the human spirit," challenge the status quo, deliver the very best while being accountable, and drive performance through the lens of humanity. They want everyone to expect more than coffee.

So if you worked for Starbucks, you'd want to be sure your values were clearly aligned with their uncompromising principles (which are posted on the company's website).

If your values include holding yourself accountable, respecting others, challenging the status quo, and being courageous, you would be in alignment. But if you don't actually believe that everyone should be welcome, or you get irritated when a rude customer takes forever ordering his double caramel macchiato with only two pumps of sugar-free vanilla syrup (instead of three), soy milk (instead of regular milk) and double caramel drizzle (instead of single), you're probably not a good fit and won't be happy working there. If you're tapping your foot, rolling your eyes, and wondering why he can't just order the drink the way in which it was intended to be served, you're probably not their ideal employee either.

Now it's your turn. To begin, look through the work you did in the first section as you developed your story, chapters, values, and dreams to find your truth. These provide hints about behaviors, thoughts, and feelings that mean the most to you.

Then reflect on your skills and strengths. Find the common themes. Are you motivated by coaching or inspiring others, is work/life balance a priority, do you want to study art or music, or are you passionate about pursuing a certain field of work you always wanted to but never did? Consider how you want to put these skills to work, what skills you might need to brush up on or learn, and then craft where you want to be in five years—that's your vision.

You'll use your journal and notes as reference when you complete the exercises at the end of this chapter.

Remember, words have power—including the words you say to yourself. Writing everything down and keeping it in a place where you can refer to it often makes it more meaningful, more real. Gone are your days of reacting to the circumstances that happen in your life and living by default. When you refer to your vision statement before taking a new course of action or before making a decision, you'll make it easier to stay true to yourself. You'll be able to avoid distractions. You'll be proactive and living on purpose, by design.

Chapter 10 Exercise A

Answering these questions will help you shape your vision and mission statements and uncover why you want this new perfect future. Be thoughtful and honest. And if other thoughts come to mind as you're answering these, jot those down too.

1. What are your five or six most important values?
2. Which personality quadrant most resonates with your ideal workday? Why?
3. If money weren't an issue and you never had to work another day in your life, how would you spend your time?
4. What five things do you most enjoy doing? What makes them enjoyable?
5. What five things must you have in your workday to finish the day feeling fulfilled? Which are missing from the workday you now have?
6. What strengths, weaknesses, talents, and skills do you see in yourself?
7. What strengths, weaknesses, talents, and skills do others see in you?
8. If you had a chance to relive your work life, at what point would you start a new chapter and choose a different path to make your work more fulfilling and enjoyable?
9. Where do your views on work and life complement each other? Where do they clash?
10. What would you most like to be remembered for when you are reminiscing about your life in your old age?

After you've crafted your personal and business vision and mission statements, lay them side by side and see where they overlap. That will give you an even better idea of where you want to go in your next chapter.

Chapter 10 Exercise B

Now dig deep again. Ask yourself one last, extremely important question.

What is my WHY?

Remember, the why is the purpose, cause, or belief that drives you. It's why you get out of bed in the morning. If you truly understand your why, you'll be able to stick with this whole idea of designing and living your dream. It will keep you in the game.

Chapter 10 Exercise C

Now think about who you want to be in 5, 10, 15, or 20 years.

1. Using your answers from the exercises you've completed, start to craft your intentions in separate vision and mission statements for your work and personal life.

   Starting with "My vision is..." craft realistic thoughts that reflect the characteristics, values, skills, and talent you identified as important. Write these statements as if you are already making them happen in your life. Don't worry about the length. Some people have a sentence and others have a paragraph. The more detailed you are in writing down your perfect future, the better you'll be able to visualize yourself living it.

2. Then take a good hard look at what you have written. Be honest with yourself. If you love working

for the company you are with right now, are your values and personal mission statement in alignment with their philosophy? If not, why? What would need to change to bring them into alignment? Do you have that written into your vision for the future?

If you're still telling yourself you're not worthy of the perfect career, you couldn't possibly spend the money to go back to school, you should be content in your current job until retirement, or you don't have what it takes to start your own business, I want you to dig deeper. Ask yourself why you feel that way. Uncover those limiting beliefs or untruths that are still holding you back and let them go.

3. Do your mission and vision statements align with your *why*? If not, what will you do to bring them into alignment?

Take your time. You're going to use this work as a foundation in establishing goals and objectives and crafting an action plan so you can start living by design—your design.

Chapter 11
Establish Your Goals ⦀

"Setting goals is the first step in
turning the invisible into the visible."

— Tony Robbins,
American author, coach, motivational
speaker, and philanthropist

*I*sn't this an interesting and amazing process? I mean,
seriously, the best part is it's all about *you* finding and
realizing *your* dreams. It encourages you to be quiet
and listen to your heart. And face it, how often do we do that in
this busy world we live in? I think not often enough. We're too
busy rushing around doing things that are oftentimes just distractions in the grand scheme of life. We've allowed the plans
and dreams of others to come before our own. We've buried
ours deep inside because others told us they were foolish.
We've been afraid.

But not anymore. You've uncovered your dreams and are well
on your way to making them reality. Your vision for the future
is your destination. Your dreams will pull you through the bad
times and days when you're feeling lost or low-vibe. You will
have bad days (we all do), and they can distract or overwhelm
you if you don't have something really purposeful to pull you
out and get you refocused.

111

You've worked hard up to this point, been thoughtful and introspective. You've thought through your life values and, with those as a foundation, turned your likes, dislikes, skills, and talents into a vision for your ideal future. You understand your why, your reason for wanting to achieve it.

Now you're going to set some goals and objectives.

These will be your compass, your guide on this journey. They translate your excitement into specific, strategic action to get what you want.

Setting goals and objectives is a powerful process for turning vision into reality. Goal setting helps you create a path to the perfect future and keeps you focused while you're taking the steps needed to get there. It supports your decision and choices you've made about what you want in your life, allows you to separate what's meaningful from mere distractions. Goals motivate you.

Ideally you should only have about five goals at any given time. You don't want so many that you become overwhelmed. And as you achieve one goal after another, you gain the self-confidence you need to be truly successful.

Your goals and objectives should be effective, achievable, and so relevant that they will pull you toward your desired future no matter what.

For best results you can follow the SMART approach, meaning each goal should be specific, measurable, attainable, relevant, and time-based.

To make it specific, ask yourself who, what, where, when, and why. Knowing how many, how much, or how you'll know when you've reached your goal will make it measurable. Knowing you have the resources (or access to the resources) to do the work will make it attainable, and making sure it's aligned with your vision, mission and values makes it relevant. Finally, you must have a specific deadline.

For example, if your goal is to get a new job, you're being way too vague. If you are intrigued with the expanding gig economy and want to start your own business to be an inspiring leader and have more flexibility and freedom, you might consider this instead.

> To achieve my goal of starting my own busi-
> ness, I will find a company that aligns with my
> vision to market my skills online or forge a path
> as a freelancer by the end of the month.

That will inspire you to take action and make sure you have accomplished the first step in defining your future within a specific timeframe.

But there are tips for setting goals with intention so you can concentrate on your efforts, stay focused, and quickly spot distractions that can get you off course. The first is to write them down. That way, they will be more meaningful and real to you. Make sure they make you feel good, they are clearly aligned with your vision, and you want to do the work to achieve them. If you're just going to go through the motions without the feel-good emotion driving you, you're just checking things off a list. Where's the fun in that?

Others are to make your feelings and excitement the heart of the matter and, as in the example above, state each goal as a positive statement. Setting a goal implies change, and change invokes fear. Your ego will try to tell you why you shouldn't be doing it, or why you should be doing it another way. It's just trying to protect you and keep you safe. But remember, your dreams are located outside your comfort zone and you have to break out, embrace change, and create new habits on this journey to your new destination.

Goals should be relevant but also realistic. Set goals that cause you to stretch outside your comfort zone, but ones you have a chance of achieving. If your goal is to be a millionaire in six months, but you don't want to lift a finger to get there because you like being a couch potato, you're not being realistic. Just sayin'.

You may not know everything you need to know to achieve them right now. You may have to do some research, read books, take a class, or gather more information in order to achieve the goal, but that's okay. In fact, it's more than okay. You always want to be learning and growing. Having achievable goals that encourage you to learn and grow will make you a stronger person in the long run.

You will have to put in the work. So make sure your goals are exciting, inspirational, and believable. Chasing meaningless ones that really don't make you happy or inspire you—or setting goals you don't believe that you (or anyone else for that matter) could achieve—will set you up for disappointment, failure, or even worse...fear. Fear blocks your creativity and action. You'll procrastinate and feel stuck. You don't want that and neither do I. It's exhausting.

Remember, you're designing a path, a journey, that will become your reality. You're designing your future. And while you have your eyes on the prize, the destination, you still live in the present, which means you can and will get curve balls thrown at you at any time. The more inspirational and believable your goals are, the more you will be able to stay focused on them and continue taking the steps you've outlined to act on them. Even when the curve balls come at you.

One way to make sure that what you've set out to accomplish is realistic and attainable is to set performance goals, not outcome goals. Performance goals are based on your personal performance, your ability to achieve that prize, and not on outside factors you have no control over.

Perhaps the best way to describe the difference is in terms of athletics. If your goal is to run the 100-meter sprint in 12.5

seconds, you have greater control in achieving this goal than winning the race because you'll undoubtedly be running alongside athletes who could potentially be faster or slower than you. So your performance goal is "Run the 100-meter sprint in 12.5 seconds." The outcome goal is winning the race. If you run the race in 12.5 seconds, you have achieved your performance goal, even if you don't get the gold medal. See how setting outcome goals could set you up for disappointment?

Let's go back to the example of your goal to get a new job. If you had written into your goal a measurement that you would be making the same amount of money after six months as someone who had been with the company for six years, you've set an outcome goal. Your success wasn't based on your performance; it was based on someone else's. If you truly believe it is possible to be making that income in six months, and after researching the possibilities have come up with a plan that's realistic and attainable, go for it.

Above all, respect both versions of yourself: where you are at the moment and where you want to be in the future. Stay in your own damn lane and enjoy your journey.

Goals establish where you intend to go. You can see the end result, which means you'll know when you get there. The more carefully you define your goals, the more likely you are to do the most effective things to achieve them. Once you have clear goals, you can break them down into more manageable steps called objectives.

Objectives are the specific steps you take in order to reach each of your goals. They specify what you must do and when. So goals tell you where you want to go and objectives tell you exactly how to get there.

Goals are typically described in words, and objectives often come with numbers and specific dates. With objectives you'll want to be precise and include timeframes and amounts so you can measure your progress. State exactly what you want to accomplish and when.

I'm an avid college football fan and a die-hard Penn Stater. In a football analogy, the goal for a player would be to score a touchdown. An objective would be to get the ball and move it through a series of plays and first downs in order to cross the goal line into the end zone.

Earlier, I used an example of a goal you might use if you were interested in starting your own business. One objective might be to research direct sales companies that sell products you might be interested in and compile that information by a certain date. You might interview successful people within the company and get their stories and advice (the good and bad). Another objective might be to explore websites or companies that might need your skills as a freelancer by a specific date.

As I've said before, one of my goals is to build a community of women who feel empowered and confident in their ability to dream, design, and live their lives on purpose and with passion in any chapter of their life. One of my objectives for that particular goal was to write this book and have it published by a certain date. Another was to have my website up and running within a specific timeframe. Both objectives were specific, measurable, and short-term.

And don't forget your financial goals and objectives. Here you want to be specific. Write out a clear, concise statement of *how much* money you intend to acquire, *when* you will have it in the bank, *what* you intend to give in return for the money, and *how* you intend to acquire it. Make your financial goals realistic and achievable too.

Now it's your turn. The next exercise will help you articulate your goals and objectives.

Chapter 11 Exercise

1. Write down your top five goals as positive, performance-based (not outcome-based) statements.
   a. Write your excitement into each goal.
   b. Make them realistic, achievable, inspiring, and believable.
   c. Push yourself outside your comfort zone with each one.

2. List at least two specific, measurable objectives for each goal.
   a. Objectives are the specific steps you take in order to reach each of your goals. They specify what you must do and by when.
   b. Objectives often come with numbers and specific dates. Be precise and include timeframes and amounts so you can measure your progress.

Congratulations! You have a vision for the future and understand why you want to pursue it. You have also clearly articulated the goals and objectives that will get you there. Now you're going to put it into action.

Chapter 12
Create Your Action Plan ‖

"A dream doesn't become reality
through magic; it takes sweat,
determination, and hard work."

— Colin Powell,
American politician, diplomat,
and retired four-star general

*U*p to this point, you've focused on *what* you want your next chapter to be based on your dreams, core values, vision, goals, and objectives.

Now it's time to roll up your sleeves and figure out *how* you're going to turn that into your new reality and how you're going to monitor your progress. The *how* is simply an action plan that includes the strategy or approach you'll use to move you closer to your goals.

Is your ego in overdrive again? Is it telling you this is all foolishness and you should just fall back into your comfort zone, even if it means living a ho-hum life of wishing away the workdays so you can make it to the weekend? Take a deep breath and keep going.

If you're thinking this process takes too much time, remember this is about creating a new, best chapter of your life. One where you want to jump out of bed with excitement every single workday. One where you are aligned with your core values. One where you are turning your dreams into reality.

This is significant. Take whatever time you need.

Let me be clear. It won't happen overnight. And it will take a lot of hard work. But if you do the work, it will be so worth it. Won't that be amazing?

As a brief review of the last chapter, a goal is a broad outcome that may take years to achieve. It is usually a brief, general statement of where you want to be or what you want to achieve. Your core values and vision are at the heart of your goals; your goals help you realize your dream by being in alignment with them. An objective is a measurable step taken toward reaching that goal. It must be specific, actionable, and measurable.

Your strategy is the foundation for the actions you take, the first step in your action plan—the thinking part—that helps you define how you will achieve your goals. Strategies are specific statements that are tied to your goals and state how you will get there.

Remember the example of a goal and objectives to start your own business from the last chapter? One objective was to research direct sales companies. So your strategy would be to identify five companies that interest you and find contact information or representatives to interview. One strategy for the freelance objective might be to identify five companies you'd be interested in providing services for. Another might be to think about how you will market your skills to those companies.

Action items are what some strategic planning gurus call tactics. They drill down into specifically *what* you will do to achieve your goals and objectives based on your strategy. They are clear, concise, and concrete—the small steps you will take every day to move you closer to what you desire. Consider strategies as the "thinking" part and your tactics as the "doing" part of your action plan.

Be sure each action item is specific. Write out what you will do, and add a target date. Make sure these action items are on your calendar.

Strategy and tactics work together as a means to an end. Just remember to think strategically and act tactically. Your action plan is your roadmap.

Action items for the first strategy should be to contact the company or representatives you identified and document your results in a spreadsheet. A follow-up action item would be to list the pros and cons of each company to help you decide the path you want to take. Action items for the second strategy should be developing a resume or letter of introduction to send to potential clients. A follow-up action would be to actually send the information and document the results in a spreadsheet.

It's incredibly important that your actions are aligned with where you want to be in the future, but equally important that you watch for and take advantage of opportunities as they happen. You wouldn't want to miss any of the magic coming your way. And those opportunities just might help you achieve your goals more quickly or more easily. I call them pivots.

Say for example you sent a resume to one of the potential clients you identified in your freelancing opportunity strategy, and the company responded with a proposal that demanded more of your time than you were expecting. Your pivot might be to make some time in the evenings and on the weekend to latch on to the opportunity and prove to them what you can do. And this might just be the start of an incredible next chapter. Remember, I started my life as an entrepreneur with one small contract; that was my pivot.

Up to this point, a lot of what you've worked on has been long-term in nature. That's what strategic thinking is really all about—being introspective but using that wisdom to plan for future events. Your action plan, and specifically your action items, are short-term efforts you take to move you closer to what you want long term.

The last part of your action plan is to monitor your progress. Take time every month to reflect on what you've done. Find a quiet place and pull out your vision, goals, objectives, strategies, and actions. Determine which actions are on track, which ones need attention, and which ones are offtrack or not in alignment with your long-term vision.

If you're offtrack, figure out why. Make any necessary course corrections to get yourself back on track. Reschedule your action items or tweak your objectives or strategies to better align with your overall goals. Manage your ego.

There's nothing wrong with adjusting your design along the way. Those are the pivots I talked about. Just make sure you are pivoting based on what you want, not what someone else thinks best for you. Don't let anyone rob you of your dreams. You have worked so hard to uncover false beliefs and get past your fear of failure or of not being good enough.

Just start! No one has all the answers in the beginning. In fact, a lot of the people you think have it together all the time are just winging it. Some may be faking it until they make it. So do it even if you're scared. Your ego doesn't know the difference between fear based on some past event and fear of pushing to a new level. It just knows fear.

Most answers will reveal themselves through action and doing, not when you're just thinking about it. So stay focused, be determined. You owe it to yourself.

And make sure to celebrate all the successes you have along the way: those milestones you hit, the actions you crossed off your to-do list, the goals you achieved.

Let me give you an example. As you may recall, one of my objectives was to get my website up and running by a certain date. A specific strategy to help me achieve this was to hire someone to build the website for me. I could have built a website myself, but I knew I didn't have enough time to learn how to do it, especially by the deadline I had set. And I knew I needed to call in the experts. So I put my creative talent to work writing the content for the website (action item) and hired someone else to do the rest. As a result, my website was up and running within three months.

Here were my action items to support this strategy:

- Find a website developer, review the contract, sign it, and pay the agreed-upon price.
- Fill out my website developer's questionnaire to guide our work together.
- Write the content according to a schedule I created.
- Complete the assignments she gave me to keep us on track.

I checked them all off. On schedule. The whole project went as smoothly as expected, and I had a website that was far superior to what I could have created on my own.

As you're working on your action plan, remember your limitations, your weaknesses. Ask for help. You'll save yourself a lot of heartache and stress.

In this chapter's exercise, you'll write down your strategies and tactics. Then you're ready to move into the final section of the book.

Chapter 12 Exercise

Develop an action plan for two or three of your objectives.
Include strategies, tactics, and timelines.

You've dreamed and designed your perfect life. Now it's time to live it. In these last few chapters, I'll give you more tools to keep you focused on and excited about your journey so you can go ahead and live it.

SECTION III

Live It

Chapter 13
Master Your Mindset ‖

*C*ongratulations! You now have clarity on your dreams and are ready to turn them into reality. You've articulated your vision, set goals and objectives, and developed strategies and specific actions to get you there. You're clear on what you want. You have a plan in place. Now it's time to take the first step in living it.

To do this, you must make a decision. Sounds easy, right? I'm not going to sugarcoat this, because the decision you make to take the leap and the level of commitment you have to follow through will make or break you.

One decision can stand in the way of your success or failure. It's not a New Year's resolution that's going to fall by the wayside as soon as the going gets tough—it's a commitment to yourself.

Decide right now to follow your dream for the life you've always wanted. Make a commitment to yourself that you will keep going no matter what. You'll keep your momentum—your eyes on that mountain—even when you're walking through the valleys and stumbling over obstacles. Believe it or not, those hurdles are there to make you stronger and help you on your journey.

So keep your focus but make the journey fun because it should be. Otherwise, what's the point?

Some people just freeze when faced with a decision. Here's an exercise you can do if that ever happens to you. Take 10 deep breaths and release all the clutter in your mind. Focus on your breathing, inhaling positive vibrations and releasing confusion, fear, doubt and worry. When you're done, think about your options and consequences. Better yet, write them down. Ask yourself whether the action you're about to take or the decision you're about to make is an escape or a solution. Then decide.

When you focus, you can approach any decision with a rational mind, which helps to relieve stress and can stop a panic attack before it ever gets started.

And again, when you feel like quitting, don't. Instead, gather lots of information so you can figure out why you're feeling that way and set yourself up to make a more informed decision. And while you're at it, pay attention to what's going on in your subconscious mind—your limiting beliefs, your ego. Because I can guarantee that if you have decided you are going to quit that job you hate and start living your dream, your ego will pitch a huge hissy fit.

The movie *True Grit* doesn't have anything to do with quitting your job, but it has a lot to do with some of the concepts I'm covering here, including determination, courage, faith, and tenacity. It demonstrates clearly what can be accomplished when you have an unwavering desire to see something through.

In the movie, 14-year-old Mattie Ross hires a tough, crotchety Deputy U.S. Marshal, Rooster Cogburn, to track down her father's murderer and bring him to justice. She hires him because she heard he has "true grit." But as you watch the scenes unfold, it becomes clear that Mattie is the one with this quality.

You have to break through any roadblocks that appear in your way instead of taking them as a sign you shouldn't be doing what you're doing. In the movie, Cogburn refuses the teenager's offer because he doubts her grit, her determination, and her ability to pay for his services. Ross raises the money in a brilliant and comical scene of horse trading where she fearlessly outwits the horse trader, ending up with not only the money but also a horse.

When a Texas Ranger and Cogburn team up to pursue the murderer and leave the teenager behind, she fearlessly pushes her new horse to swim across a river to catch up with the pair. She continues to show her true grit by interrogating outlaws, confronting and killing her father's murderer to keep from being attacked, and surviving a rattlesnake bite that results in her forearm being amputated. (I was doing the snake dance!)

That's true grit. Find yours. You'll need it.

Growing into your dreams can seem painful at times. But it's far less painful than living life by default. If you want to pursue and live a life of your dreams, take control and stop at nothing. Be Mattie Ross, even if your ego goes into overdrive and your friends tell you you're crazy. Stay the course. Let everyone stare in awe when you transform your life into something amazing.

So make the decision. Commit to it. Gather lots of information along the way. Stick to it.

During the messy time after I left my corporate job, one thing that helped me gain clarity and confidence was getting into the right mindset. Instead of agonizing over what I no longer had, I turned my attention to the opportunities. I thought about who I was without limitations, my values, what strengths and talent I wanted to apply moving forward, and what I wanted to leave behind. Those reminders alone moved me from a lack mentality to one of abundance. Once I made that switch, the ideas came easily and I became excited about the possibilities.

Shifting your mindset takes practice. It doesn't happen overnight. It's not a destination, which means you must always be aware of your thoughts and feelings and be willing to pivot when you find yourself on the wrong path.

But you must have the right mindset if you're going to start pursuing your dreams according to your design. You've come so far. You know you're meant for more. I know you are too.

Still, you need to find a method that works for you. Some people spend quiet time with God, their Creator, the Universe, or their source. Others meditate, journal, or engage energy healers.

I'll touch on each of these in later chapters, but let's start with the one that meant the most to me. I was raised in a Christian home. Weekly worship (sometimes several times a week) was a part of my life growing up. I believed in God. I believed He had a plan for me.

But once I graduated high school and was out on my own, I didn't worship in the same way. I still believed in God, but I didn't put Him front and center of my life. And I certainly didn't ask for guidance as I should have. Had I done so, my blood pressure wouldn't have been through the roof like it so often was. I would have been able to weather life's storms much better than I did. I would have been able to focus more on the positive aspects of my life, to be grateful, and in the process drown out the negative.

Now here's a lesson I learned in my mess: The closer I got to God, the more I trusted in Him and in myself, the more I was grateful for what I had rather than focusing on what I lacked, the more at peace I was. That's what I had been taught years ago. Guess I'm just a slow learner sometimes.

But once I figured out where I'd gone wrong and how I could get back on track to find comfort and peace, I also had to forgive myself and let it go. Forgiveness gives you peace. You stop being a captive to any resentment or grudges you may have, and you can start to focus on other things that are more productive. Whether it is courage or fairness, forgiveness gives you strength over any situation.

But when you are filled with anger and resentment over past misdeeds, you cannot really understand this. You can only accept it when you are willing to forgive the past, let go, and move on. You are responsible for your actions and the decisions you make. Make them based on the direction you want to take and what will serve in your best interest, not on regret, resentment, or a mistake you made.

Because face it, everyone makes mistakes. Those failures remind you that you are perfectly imperfect, just like everyone else. Forgive yourself so you can live without fear or regret. Once you do, you'll begin to see yourself as a student of life. You'll start seeing possibilities and become more positive, even in the face of wrongdoings and misgivings. You can be more tolerant and less bitter, and live better.

Now let me add a small disclaimer here. You see, I'm faithful but also full of flaws. You may have seen the phrase "I love Jesus, but I swear a little." I like wine. I swear a little. I drive over the speed limit sometimes. I'm perfectly imperfect. And I'm okay with that. I'm human, just like you.

So accept that you have flaws. You're going to make mistakes and have setbacks. You're going to have times of doubt and negative self-talk. Because we all do.

Assess. Make adjustments. Get in the right mindset. Move on. Don't ever give up on your dreams. It's not an option.

Now it's your turn. As you go through this final section, connect with your higher source or do whatever you must do to tap into your true grit. Keep in mind that you're perfectly imperfect, and remember the importance of gratitude and forgiveness as you complete the exercises. That will give you the foundation for living life by design.

Chapter 13 Exercise

1. Think about the last decision you made. Were you indecisive or frozen with fear?
2. Imagine you were faced with that same decision today.
3. Try the Get Clear exercise.
   a. Take 10 deep breaths and release all the clutter in your mind.
   b. Focus on your breathing, inhaling positive vibrations and releasing confusion, fear, doubt, and worry.
   c. When you're done, think about your options and consequences. Better yet, write them down.
   d. Ask yourself whether the action you're about to take or the decision you're about to make is an escape or a solution. Then decide.
4. Were you able to better focus? Get clarity? Were you able to think rationally without fear? Were you able to tap into your true grit?

Next, you'll learn about universal laws that create balance and harmony in nature and how you can tap into them to create your best life.

Chapter 14
Tap Into Universal Laws ‖‖‖

"One man's woo-woo, of course, is
another's deeply held belief system."

— Julia Moskin,
New York Times

*I*t's human nature to believe mostly in the things we
can see, feel, taste, hear, or touch and to doubt everything else. But our nonphysical being—our inner self
or mind—houses things we cannot see yet still believe in.
Universal laws that create balance and harmony in nature are
also at play in our lives. Even though we can't see them, if we
can tap into and believe in them, we can use them to create our
best life.

Just a few years ago, I would have said these laws were woo-
woo and perhaps even voodoo. I would have said the same
thing about the Ouija board and calculus. Oh, and maybe
some of the Stephen King movies like *It* and *Christine*. No,
maybe they were more like nightmares. Now that I think about
it, calculus was voodoo and a nightmare all rolled into one.
Just sayin'.

Twelve universal laws or principles govern the Universe and
allow it to exist in perfect harmony. I'm going to focus on three

for purposes of designing your next chapter: Law of Vibration, Law of Attraction, and Law of Inspired Action.

The Law of Vibration (the foundation for the other two) refers to energy and states that anything that exists in our Universe, whether seen or unseen, consists of pure energy or light that resonates and exists as a vibratory frequency.

If you took physics or chemistry, you undoubtedly learned that energy is the capacity for doing work. As part of the Law of Conservation of Energy, it can be neither created nor destroyed, but only changed from one form to another.

Think about fire, for example: a chemical reaction that combines the molecules in wood with oxygen from the air to create water and carbon dioxide. The molecules aren't destroyed, they just change. And as they vibrate and transform, they release energy in the form of heat and light.

Everything in the Universe moves and vibrates at some speed. So that energy, in you and in everything around you, is moving all the time. Each matter, thought, and feeling has its own vibrational frequency. And that means the words we say to ourselves, thoughts and feelings we choose to have, and actions we take as a result also have their own particular rates of vibration.

Author Esther Hicks contends that these vibrations—and ultimately who we are—are simply extensions of source energy, which flows through everything. Now I happen to believe this source is God and that He created the Universe. But these universal laws work for everyone, regardless of religious beliefs. So you can call your source anything you like: Creator, light, broader intelligence, a unicorn, or the Universe itself. Just like in physics, energy can be neither created nor destroyed but only changed from one form to another. According to Hicks, energy transfers from the source to us.

So if we're simply extensions of source energy, we somehow must attract that energy, right? Yep, we do—in our thoughts.

You see, everything starts with a thought. That thought creates a belief, and that belief has emotion or feelings attached. Emotion is our inner GPS system, and our thoughts are attracting from a source through energetic vibrations.

Source energy vibrates at a high frequency. Positive thoughts and emotions have a higher frequency than negative ones. So if you're stuck in a place you don't want to be, you might consider your part in that. Perhaps your thoughts and emotions are negative ones that you have chosen over the higher, positive vibrations your source is trying to send your way.

When I was living out of boxes, my thoughts and emotions were definitely low frequency. I felt lost, clinging to a past life. I robbed myself of the excitement of searching for a new home and designing that space—something I had thoroughly enjoyed before. My source was sending positive vibrations, reassurances that everything would be all good soon, but I deflected them like Luke Skywalker with a lightsaber and blast shield. My life turned out to be better than expected. The months I spent worrying about it were a waste of time and energy.

Instead of drowning out my enthusiasm, what if I had expected the Universe and my source to support my dream to have a home as nice or better than the one I had just sold? One that was in the perfect community with people just waiting to become friends and neighbors? One that was nice enough, but was just waiting for that special someone to make it perfect? Because that's what happened. But if I had opened my mind to the possibilities early on, I would have been able to deflect worry, doubt, and fear, raise my frequency, and embrace excitement and the journey.

If you turn your negative thoughts into positive ones, you'll open your mind up to more desirable options and a perfect solution. Expect the Universe and your source to support your dream and it will. Just remember to raise your frequency so you can communicate on the same level.

Another universal law, the one most recognized today, and the one that holds the Universe together according to some, is the Law of Attraction. It states that from the words you speak to the beliefs you have, you attract everything in your life through energy. It's based on the laws of attractive and repulsive force, the idea that like attracts like.

So whether it's negative or positive, everything you have in your life is what you've attracted. And that includes the people in your life because they have the same energy frequency as you. Have you ever been introduced to someone who instantly became your best friend? You laugh at the same jokes, like the same foods, and share the same outlook on life. Chances are it's because you share the same energy frequency.

Understanding this law is essential to feeling joyful and being fulfilled, and that leads to a life filled with passion and purpose. I believe that most of us are seeking joy in life. So if you're happy and optimistic, you're operating at that higher energy vibration. You'll be drawn to others on the same frequency and attract more of the positive outcome in your life.

But what happens when you're around people who aren't on your frequency? Because, let's face it, not everyone is happy. We all know people who are all doom and gloom. I like to call them Mr. Miserable based on the children's book *Mr. Happy* by Roger Hargreaves. If you're not familiar with the story, Mr. Happy lives in Happyland, a place where even animals and plants are happy. On a walk, he meets someone who looks just like him but doesn't act like him. He's Mr. Miserable. Demonstrating his positive attitude, Mr. Happy is able to turn his grumpy new friend around.

No one wants to be around a Mr. Miserable day in and day out. It's sure to drag your positive vibrational energy down. So if you have people like this in your life, try being positive, happy, and joyful. It's contagious. You may turn them around and change lives. And if you can't, you may have to consider options to protect your energy vibration. Unfriend them on social media. Stop meeting them at the coffee shop. Leave that tribe and find a new circle of high-vibe friends to hang out with. You owe it to yourself.

Perhaps this quote (sometimes attributed to John Lennon) said it best.

> When I was five years old, my mother always told me that happiness was the key to life. When I went to school, they asked me what I wanted to be when I grew up. I wrote down "happy." They told me I didn't understand the assignment, and I told them they didn't understand life.

Be happy so you attract happy.

According to leading authors on this topic, the Law of Attraction has always been in existence and its concepts are rooted in some religious beliefs. Buddha said, "All that we are is the result of what we have thought. The mind is everything. What we think, we become." In the Bible, Galatians 5:6, we see a similar thought: "Whatsoever a man soweth, that shall he also reap." And again in Matthew 21:22: "And all things, whatsoever ye shall ask in prayer, believing, ye shall receive."

The ancient Greeks knew from the observation of magnetics that opposites attract and likes repel. The first known usage of the term *Law of Attraction*, however, is attributed to Helena Blavatsky. In her book written in 1877, Blavatsky says, "The Universe is worked and guided from within outwards." She was telling us that we have the power *within* us to influence what happens *to* us.

The Law of Attraction became more popular and influential a century later, when Jerry and Esther Hicks rose to prominence with nine books, collectively called *The Teachings Of*

Abraham, in which they professed to channel messages from nonphysical beings.

You might think channeling messages from nonphysical beings is a bit like voodoo, but I often say my Bouvier puppy, Alli, is channeling messages and actions that my other, now-departed dogs used to display. One of my favorites is when she knows you're about to peel a banana and comes running for a bite. That's when she's channeling Jacmel. When she's chasing deer or her prey instincts are in overdrive, she's channeling Kaya, who was hell on wheels when it came to gophers or deer. So yes, I believe in channeling. That shit is real in my world.

In 2006, Rhonda Byrne's documentary film and subsequent book *The Secret* brought the Law of Attraction front and center to a worldwide audience. Through conversations with leading scientists, authors, doctors, and philosophers, Byrne shared how to intentionally create a life of everything you've ever wanted, including joy, abundance, well-being, peace, and love. The movie emphasizes how learning new ways of thinking, recognizing and curbing negative thoughts, and setting goals are all key to getting what you really want.

This is exactly what I've been talking about. Eliminating the negative self-talk, doubt, fear, and worry. The lowest point on the emotional scale is fear, grief, and pessimism. Doubt, worry, and limiting beliefs are at the midrange. So if something doesn't feel good, that's an indication that you need to move yourself up the vibrational ladder. When you're feeling joyful, calm, hopeful, and loving, you're at a higher vibration and you'll attract what you want.

So this concept has been around for a very long time in a variety of forms. But how exactly does the Law of Attraction work? Source energy is physical energy, but it is also nonphysical in the form of thoughts, beliefs, and feelings. Thankfully, as humans we have the ability to be acutely aware of both, and because of this, we can consciously connect with our source.

When you get a new idea, source energy first acts vibrationally (non-physically through thoughts and feelings), then eventually that idea becomes physical manifestation. For example, if you've decided on a particular job based on your values and Zone of Genius and you're truly excited about it, those emotions become nonphysical vibrations that motivate you to take action. You'll visualize yourself in that new position, set goals and milestones to help you get there, and do the work to manifest what you want. You're excited and positive about the journey. By adjusting your thoughts and feelings, you can adjust the outcome of your life.

Most people pay attention to their thoughts, but I'd offer that it's better to pay attention to your emotions. When you do this, you will understand whether you are positively attracting what you want or negatively attracting what you don't want. You'll know that because of the way you *feel*. When you are thinking about something you want, you will feel positive emotions; when you're thinking about something you don't want, you'll feel negative emotions.

This is remarkably powerful, especially during stressful, fearful, and uncertain times. If you've ever been furloughed or forced into an early retirement because of an economic downturn or recession, you may have felt confused, worried, scared, or depressed. Those are symptoms of a lack mentality. And when you're thinking about what you don't have (what you lack), you cannot attract abundance.

Instead of thinking that you don't have the skills (or degree) to find a different job, let alone pursue the job you've always dreamed of having, consider it a window of opportunity to identify the skills you do have that are relevant, figure out how you learn the rest, and explore the options that come your way (or go after ones you want to come your way). That puts you in a higher, more positive energy level where your source—your broader nonphysical energy—resides and where together you can make it happen.

Above all else, pay attention to your words, because what you tell yourself—the words you use—sets the stage for thoughts, emotions, and actions.

And remember to get creative. Focus your thoughts on where you want to be, not what your reality is today. Decide what you want, then change your vibration and your story. Think of it like programming yourself just like you would the navigation system on your car. When you want to go to that new restaurant, you enter the address into your navigation system and the guide gives you step-by-step driving directions. When you want to manifest a new job or career, you need to program the steps you will take—the directions—in your mind to keep you focused and excited about the destination.

Remember, you're following your dreams. So consider this: What you desire and what God, the Universe, or whatever source you believe in desires for you are not at odds. And that source does not distinguish between a thought brought about by your observation of reality and a thought brought about by your imagination. If you focus on either one long enough, it will *become* your reality. That next chapter you're designing is a perfect example. If you follow your plan, stay connected to your source, and operate at a high frequency, you will have a new reality.

But to follow your plan, you must act. And that leads me to the Law of Inspired Action, which says we must take action whenever we want to accomplish something, even if we are operating at a higher vibrational level and paying attention to our thoughts and feelings. We are physical beings on a physical planet, but we must do more than just think and visualize. We need to put those perpetual wheels in motion.

So you now have a desire for creating and living your dream, and you know how to ask the Universe to make it happen. Congratulations! People don't often get that far.

Many people spend their days exchanging some sort of action or service for money. In the past, my workday started with a 5 am alarm and usually a groan. It became so hard to wake up with positive thoughts, let alone joy and passion, when I knew I'd soon be hit with the negativity of the day. I suspect you also want to trade that drudgery for a profession that involves money but also involves joy. You can.

But before you launch into action to get the things you want, you must have the right mindset, as I've said many times. Catch yourself when you have negative thoughts like:

- I'm not good enough.
- What if I fail?
- What will other people think?

Knock that off right now. It won't serve you at all in creating a life of your dreams.

Start trusting yourself. Stop listening so much to others telling you what to do, what you shouldn't do, what is right, and what is wrong. This is your life. Assuming you're not doing anything against the law or unethical, you have the right to create a workday that leaves you fulfilled and happy.

An effective way to turn a negative thought into a positive one and raise the frequency at the same time is to change the subject altogether. Deliberately look for the positive aspect of what you are thinking and focus on that. Think the positive thoughts into being—see them, visualize them, expect them—and they will be. From this state of positive thinking, you'll be inspired to act. But instead of drudgery, it will be coming from a place of joy.

And while you're at it, practice gratitude, because nothing will bring instant joy into your life more than focusing on things you are grateful for. Gratitude means you are operating from a point of strength and good. You are pushing positive thoughts to the forefront and shutting out thoughts of fear, failure, and negativity.

By giving positive thought to what you want, you are inviting it into your world, you are attracting and creating it—by design and on purpose. You are focusing on a solution, which results in feeling good.

Doing this could really change your life.

Now what if you're doing all this, but what you've asked the Universe for hasn't happened yet? It's not happening according to your timing. Be okay with that. Because the other part of this equation is that even with the right mindset and the right actions, everything will happen in divine timing or as it should. And if you aren't getting exactly what you asked for and what you've taken action on, it could mean that something even better is coming your way.

When I thought the world was coming to an end and I looked around at the boxes surrounding me like a fortress, I should have known that God was planning something better than what I could ever imagine. I should have known that greater things were coming my way when I left my corporate life the first time with only one small contract and a Bouvier des Flandres as an office mate. I just needed to have patience and trust that the awesomeness was on its way.

If you feel impatient because something you want is slow to come to you, it might be because you are spending more time focused on its absence than its presence. Your thoughts are coming from a lack mentality rather than an abundance mentality.

I know that it's hard sometimes to think about better circumstances if you don't know where you'll get the money to pay your rent let alone start a business.

That's exactly where I was. Stuck, focused on what was lacking in my life—career, dream home, purpose. But once I reprogramed my internal navigation system and focused on what I wanted to do in my next chapter, I was able to turn that into abundance and purpose. By changing your thoughts and words, you can too.

You see, where you are right now has nothing to do with your current circumstances or problems, no matter how dire they seem today. You thought those problems into becoming your reality. You may think you're a victim of your circumstances; I think you are a victim of your interpretation of your circumstances.

The good news is that you can also think of solutions, which become your new reality. One way to do that is to be grateful for the progress you are making toward your next chapter. You've got a plan to start that new business now, and you have action steps to take every day. That's a great start! And I can guarantee you that if you have your plan in place and you are in action every day, you will be moving toward your dream life. Be grateful and celebrate every little step of the journey.

No more living by default or staying mired in negative thoughts for you, my friend. You were meant for more, remember?

So let's recap. All energy vibrates at a certain frequency. Vibration attracts like vibration. Positive thoughts and emotions have a higher frequency than negative ones. The nonphysical part of you vibrates on a high frequency and connects to the broader nonphysical source energy, whatever you call it.

Stay positive, because you're manifesting everything that comes into your life based on your thoughts, and you want what's coming your way to be positive and in sync with your goals.

When you learn to consciously master the energetic realm, believe in the not-yet-seen, and stay in your highest frequency, you harness your innate power to create the reality you desire.

Chapter 14 Exercise

1. Review your action plan. Now's the time to start implementing it.

2. As you look at your plan and start to write tasks and milestones on your calendar, consider these questions:

   a. What negative thoughts are creeping in?

   b. What are you going to commit to doing to check yourself before you wreck yourself?

   c. How will you move from the lowest point on the emotional scale where you are feeling fear, grief, and pessimism through the midrange point of doubt, worry, and limiting beliefs to that higher energetic vibration where you're feeling joy, calm, hope, and love?

3. Do this for about three days and see if you can identify any recurring themes.

In the next chapter, you'll learn one way you can train your mind to focus on what you want instead of inviting what you don't want into your life.

Chapter 15
Learn To Affirm ⦀

"Affirmations are like prescriptions
for certain aspects of yourself
you want to change."

— Jerry Frankhauser,
author

*Y*ou might be saying, "Okay, Christine. I think I get the whole universal law thing, but how do I actually implement it?"

One way to implement the Law of Attraction is through affirmations. When you affirm something, you are declaring it to be true. That's pretty straightforward, don't you think?

An affirmation has the ability to program your mind for the positive outcome you desire regardless of whether it's your reality at the moment.

What? Yep, we've already established that the mind is a truly incredible thing and there are ways we can control it. Remember all you learned about the conscious and subconscious parts of your mind and the logical and artistic sides of your brain?

Your mind doesn't know the difference between what is real and what is just a part of your dream or vision for the future.

The mind can imagine something that doesn't exist and it can envision circumstances that are different from the current reality. Um...like your dreams perhaps? Yep. And the good news is that you are in the driver's seat.

Is this just more woo-woo? Nope. According to a 2014 study by Geoffrey L. Cohen and David K. Sherman, people have a basic need to maintain personal integrity and adequacy. Circumstances and events that threaten that basic need cause stress that can interfere with personal growth and performance. They concluded that affirmations, particularly if aimed at core personal values, provided an intervention that was shown to improve education, health, and relationship outcomes.

To me, these threats sound a lot like ego and fear working to keep you safe. But affirmations that are firmly aligned with your core personal values, the vision you have for a better future, and your goals can intervene and help you move outside your comfort zone to the magic. These properly aligned affirmations help you ditch the negative beliefs so you can focus on the positive, perfect next chapter you've dreamed and designed.

David Schechter, a pioneer in integrating mind and body techniques for treating stress and chronic pain, uses journaling and affirmations as part of his treatment plan. He teaches patients how to use positive affirmations to counteract negative thoughts and limiting beliefs to avoid anxiety. Just as people do repetitive physical exercise to build muscle strength, focusing on the positive through affirmations is a way of reprogramming the brain. According to Schechter, affirmations can help us stop bad habits such as limiting beliefs and self-sabotage.

Schechter's study shows that our brains have the ability to form and reorganize connections, which means they can be rewired through neuroplasticity. During this rewiring, we can also delete certain connections and ultimately change the way our brains work.

Studying a foreign language is a great example of the brain's ability to rewire. I took French in both high school and college. By repeating and practicing the language, I was restructuring the connections in my brain. And I knew that all my study had paid off when I was able to...

> ...get an A on my final exam (over Skype) because I was able to clearly explain how to make West Indian roti.
>
> ...secure an affordable, reliable rental car in Martinique.
>
> ...explain to a hotel manager in Paris that my sister-in-law had locked herself in the bathroom and we couldn't figure out how to get her out.
>
> ...explain to the same hotel manager that we needed four more sets of towels because there were five of us sharing the same room.

Mais oui! I think I rewired my brain quite well, thank you very much. And I'm doing the same with my affirmations, which I'll share later.

Your words have energy and power. You've probably heard the saying "If you can't say anything nice, don't say anything at all." Did you think that only referred to words you said to someone else? What about words you say to yourself?

In reality, the most crucial communication you have is with yourself. What you tell yourself is just as powerful as what you say to others—positive or negative, out loud or quietly. Your words become thoughts. Thoughts become emotions. Emotions determine your actions. If you're telling yourself you're too old, aren't smart enough, or don't have the skills to pursue your dreams, you're programming your brain to believe it.

Try saying you deserve to pursue your dreams at any age, you are smart enough, and you either have the skills or you're excited about learning new ones. See how that makes you feel.

When you do that, your brain will take you down a different, more desirable path.

Practicing positive affirmations increases the likelihood that you can turn limiting beliefs into positive thoughts, actions, and feelings. The more you repeat something to yourself, the more your brain believes it, and the more likely you are to take action because you are in a higher vibrational state and you already believe it's possible.

When you affirm something, you are declaring it to yourself and the Universe as the truth. When this happens, your reticular activating system (RAS) kicks in. This filter sorts through the roughly eight billion pieces of information your subconscious is bombarded with at any given moment, lets in the information you need, and filters out what you don't.

When you repeat affirmations based on what matters to you over and over, your RAS lets that information in, because it's telling the brain, "This is important—pay attention!" And if your affirmations are clearly aligned with your vision, your RAS also gets busy noticing ways to help you achieve that. In the process, it also filters out the limiting beliefs because you aren't affirming them. (And if you are—stop!)

For example, one of my limiting beliefs was that I was too old to complete my degree, but I kept affirming that I would not only obtain my degree from Penn State's World Campus, I would also graduate with honors. Even when I faced challenges, my affirmative thoughts kept telling my brain to pay attention because this was important. It helped me find creative solutions to problems like where to set up my chemistry lab (the kitchen counter was perfect), and how to weave in a trip to the Caribbean to complete my renewable energy internship (Martinique, *c'est magnifique*). Even when I was tired, my affirmation was wiring my brain to keep going until I graduated with honors. That's how your RAS can kick in and help you accomplish your goals.

These positive affirmations will also go to work while you sleep. Your body needs to rest, but only half your brain rests along with your body. The other half runs your bodily functions, which includes storing all the memories of the day. Think of it as returning or adding books to the giant library system called your mind. That's why sleep is not only vital to your physical body but also to your cognitive abilities. And it's also the reason you should end your day with positive thoughts.

How exactly does it work? Let's say you desire a new house. You affirm, "I am enjoying my perfect home." You visualize it, bask in all the details of the architecture, neighborhood, landscape, floorplan, and furniture. Imagine how you'll feel in it.

But remember, you have to take action. So determine your path—the steps you will take to get there. Some steps may be to figure out how you'll get the down payment, determine which financial institution has the best interest rate, cruise neighborhoods of interest, look at houses and schools, check houses for sale online, and find a realtor.

I mentioned that one of my goals is to build a community of women who feel empowered and confident in their ability to dream, design, and live their lives on purpose and with passion in any chapter of their life. Here are some of my affirmations:

- I have the right mindset.
- I am bold and courageous.
- I trust in God's plan for me.
- I am the coauthor of my life, and I am designing my chapters and contents with God's guidance.
- I quickly rise against every negative thought and limiting belief.
- I accomplish great things.
- My book was completed on schedule and is empowering and inspiring women to dream, design, and live their lives on purpose and with passion.
- My online course is changing lives.

Notice how they're all stated in the positive and in present tense, as if they are already true.

Take the first affirmation as an example. If I said, "I need to have the right mindset," I would be focusing on my current lack of it and I would be setting my energetic vibration toward the negative. When I shift the energy to "I have the right mindset," I can visualize that I already have it, and that's the positive energetic vibrational match I'm looking for.

So be careful that you affirm what you do want instead of what you don't. If you keep affirming what you don't want, you're really just inviting it into your life.

Let's say, for example, that your business isn't growing as quickly as you would like. If you say, "My business is growing more slowly than I expected," you are reinforcing and affirming that this is okay and the negative pattern will likely continue. Shift it to something like, "I am taking the steps every day in my business to achieve and surpass my goals."

Also, saying, "My business is growing more slowly than I expected" can get you on that worrying train quicker than anything else, nothing good will come of it, and it's a total waste of time and energy. Nothing has ever been solved by worrying about it. Wringing your hands and using precious brain power fretting about what might happen in the future is futile; it robs you of today and keeps you from tapping into possibilities and solutions. It puts you on the low vibrational scale. If you find yourself on that path, please stop, pivot, and focus on the positive. It's a much better use of your valuable resources.

Some say it takes 21 days of repetition for an affirmation to start taking hold. Personally, I don't think you can put a time limit on it, because it takes a lot to rewire something as complex as your brain. And remember, ego is going to be at work trying to sabotage your efforts. Not because it doesn't want you to succeed; it's just trying to protect you. So when your mind is telling you, "It's too hard" or "I don't have enough time to do that" or "Let's just stay where we are," know that it's just your ego talking.

You'll battle your ego every time a negative thought worms its way in. The secret is to consciously choose to turn those into positive affirmations based on your dreams, vision, and goals. Repeat them as often as you need to until you've won the verbal tennis match you're having with your ego on the court and your positive thoughts cry victory. Game. Set. Match. And while you're at it, throw in a couple of aces.

Chapter 15 Exercise

1. Write down some affirmations that will program in your mind the positive outcome you desire regardless of whether or not it's your reality at the moment.

2. What will you tell yourself to counter negative thoughts and limiting beliefs?

3. Refer to all the work you've done to this point and state it as if it were already true. For example, to keep you in the right mindset, your affirmation may be, "I have the right mindset to live life by design."

4. Write them down.

5. Post them where you can see them.

6. Read them aloud every day, and more often if needed.

Affirmations help you make and visualize a change. And action gets you there. Next you'll learn how important your physical and mental health are in living this dream life you've created.

Chapter 16
Nurture Your Health ‖

*Y*ou're going to be rather busy turning the life you've dreamed and designed into reality. To be successful with what you're trying to do here, you need to be on top of your game with regard to your health. You need to think clearly and have a physical body that will cooperate, one that isn't stressed out.

I'm not going to tell you that you need to be a certain weight, you need to go on a diet, or you need to exercise like a maniac. That's really up to you. This chapter is about the importance of paying attention to your mental and physical health, whatever that means to you.

As for me, I'm not into spending every night at the gym or my money on diets that promise I'll lose 20 pounds in seven days. First, I am comfortable with my weight. Besides that, I live with a fabulous chef and I love to eat the meals he prepares. So I'm not likely to go on some diet that includes shakes and pills. Nutrition, physical activity, sleep, and stress management all contribute to a healthy lifestyle, and your body is that miracle machine where it all comes together. When any of these are out of balance, your health pays the price.

Remember check yourself before you wreck yourself? It matters here too.

Only you can figure out what that balance is. You have to decide what good nutrition means to you, what physical activity makes moving your body fun instead of total drudgery, how much sleep your body needs, and how you manage the stress in your life.

Let's start with a healthy diet. What you put in your mouth provides your body's cells with the nutrients they need to perform their functions correctly. When you don't eat healthy, nutritious food, metabolic processes slow down dramatically and your physical health declines. Eating well has key long-term consequences, but it also helps you feel more energetic and optimistic in the short term.

Healthy eating also puts you in a higher vibration state that is more positive and optimistic so you're more open to attracting what you want.

If right about now you're getting ready to clean out the pantry and rid the freezer of the gallons of ice cream you've stockpiled, hold on a minute. I'm sure you've heard the saying, "Everything in moderation." I truly believe that. There are certain food items I just can't keep in my house. If they're there, they call to me... not just once, but repeatedly until I give in. Those unhealthy food choices stay safely on the shelf in the grocery store.

For example, a bag of Cheetos always calls to me. I can walk confidently past them in the grocery store, but as soon as they are in my house, all bets are off. So it's a rare occasion when they land in my pantry. But when they do, I know I'll finish the bag in about a week and then I'm done for quite a while. That's my way of controlling something I know isn't really good for me.

If there's something you just can't pass up and you're eating way more than you should, no need to purge it, just use common sense. Figure out how to manage it for the sake of your health.

Healthy eating means getting the right nutrients through a variety of fruits and vegetables of many colors, whole grains and starches, good fats, and lean proteins. A healthy diet also means avoiding foods with high amounts of added salt and sugar.

Micronutrients, vitamins, and minerals such as iron, vitamin A, vitamin D, iodine, folate, and zinc are also vital in maintaining good health. While they are only required in small amounts, they are not produced in the body and thus must be acquired through diet. A lack of certain vitamins and minerals such as vitamin B12, calcium, and iron can also contribute to feelings of negativity and depression.

Ultimately, poor nutrition contributes to many diseases, including obesity, diabetes, heart disease, and cancer. But a healthy diet supports your immune system, so it's easier for your body to fight off colds, the flu, or other health issues. And it helps control stress too.

Let's start with breakfast. Some people believe that a cup of coffee is all they need. But studies show that skipping breakfast can lead to poor physical and intellectual health. A healthy breakfast that includes good carbohydrates and protein contributes to better concentration and performance. It also prevents atherosclerosis, which leads to increased blood pressure, higher cholesterol, chance of stroke, insulin resistance, and weight gain.

If you're a coffee-only type of gal and you are wondering why you can't seem to focus or why you have a headache, maybe it's time to rethink your breakfast routine. I've never really been a big breakfast fan unless it includes eggs. Or give me some leftovers from last night's dinner and I'm in heaven. But that's just me.

Did you ever hear the theory "After eight, gain weight" which refers to the idea that you shouldn't eat after 8:00 pm? The U.S. Department of Agriculture says it doesn't matter what time of day you eat that determines your weight, but what and how much you eat and how much physical activity you have during the day. So the 8:00 pm curfew is a false theory. Calories in versus calories out is what counts. If you're consuming sugar and fat instead of healthy vegetables and lean protein, your body will be worse off in the long run, regardless of when you consume the calories.

Along with healthy eating comes healthy drinking. No I'm not talking about alcohol, soda, or sugary drinks. (Although I will say that if you're having a beer for breakfast, you might want to reread the sections on stress and depression. Just sayin'.) I'm talking about making sure you drink enough water every day. On average, the human body consists of 60% water, which our billions of cells need to survive.

In the past, you were probably told to drink eight eight-ounce glasses of water a day. Today, it's about 3.2 quarts for an adult male and 2.3 quarts for an adult female every day. The amount of water you need will vary depending on the amount of exercise you get, the environment in which you live, and your overall health. The idea is to avoid getting dehydrated, so if you're sweating during your exercise routine because it's hot and humid outside, or because you're battling a fever, you should drink more water. Listen to your body. If you feel thirsty or sleepy or have a dry mouth, headaches, or muscle weakness, you might be dehydrated, so head on over to the water fountain.

The bottom line is that eating nutritious meals regularly gives you the energy you need to accomplish what you've set out to do to live a happy, balanced, and fulfilled life. You can't attract all the positive things you want if you haven't fueled your body properly.

So figure out what makes sense for you and look out for your health. You're the one in charge. Just remember, you only get one body. Take care of it.

Along with properly fueling your body comes the need to actually move it!

Aerobic exercise triggers the release of endorphins, potent brain chemicals that have the ability to relieve pain and stress, stimulate relaxation, and turn bad moods into good ones. Over the long term, if you exercise every day, this can even help combat depression. Simply put, the higher your level of endorphins, the greater your sense of calm and well-being.

This doesn't mean you have to train for a marathon. Just walking 20 to 30 minutes a day can make a real difference in reducing stress. So when you feel stress levels rising, take a few minutes to get your body moving. It will do wonders.

If you have a canine family member like I do, it's easier to take those walks. They deserve it and so do you. Every morning as part of my morning routine, my husband and I take Alli for a walk around the neighborhood. We do it again right before dinner. Sometimes, if I'm particularly stressed out or mulling over a problem, I'll take her for a walk at lunchtime.

Exercise is good for decluttering the mind. So find what works for you. Buy a gym membership, go for a walk in nature, take that bicycle out for a spin. Dance it up in ballroom, ballet, or hip-hop style with others, or in your living room. Just move your body.

Exercise will take you from being stuck to inspired, and from having a problem to finding a solution. You'll find that you look at things from a different perspective when you tap into your inner resources and listen to your head and your heart. You'll ditch the bad mood, stress, and foggy brain in favor of a pleasant mood, clarity, and feeling good about yourself. That's what those endorphins can do for you.

Be sure to put those endorphins to rest each day though, because getting adequate sleep is also vital in maintaining good health. Lack of adequate sleep contributes to many of the chronic diseases I've already mentioned such as diabetes, heart disease, obesity, and depression.

A third of US adults report that they usually get less than the recommended amount of sleep. But it's not just sleep, it's *quality* sleep. Studies have found that disrupted or restless sleep increases the risk of cardiovascular disease, hypertension, diabetes, and some forms of cancer. It can also sabotage your efforts to maintain your ideal weight. So be sure you get your z's.

And be sure you're not hitting that snooze button.

I never was a morning person. According to my mom, I've been a night owl since I was born. My fondest story is about when I was around one or two, sitting in the middle of the card table on pinochle night at a late hour when most babies were fast asleep.

But I never really understood the connection between being a night owl and the way you wake up until a couple of years ago when I started waking up most days with a "foggy brain." It took me a while to figure it out, but it turned out that the underlying cause was the snooze button.

Apparently hitting it even one time affects how you wake up and, along with that, your ability to be focused, positive, and productive. Interestingly enough, it all starts the night before, just as you are falling asleep.

The moment you fall asleep, you begin one of several sleep cycles. Each one lasts around 90 minutes. A couple of hours before your body starts to wake up, your core temperature increases, which makes your mind start to wake up and feel more alert and less sleepy. If you hit the snooze button for that extra 10 or 15 minutes of rest you think you'll get, you're really just confusing the mind and body wake-up mechanisms already at play.

You're saying, "Wait, no—I'm going back to sleep." The parts of your brain responsible for physiological functions respond rather quickly to that declaration, so the half of the brain that rests with the body falls back asleep. But the parts of the brain responsible for putting the information back on the library shelves, making decisions, paying attention, being alert, and exhibiting self-control—your subconscious—can't respond as quickly. It takes longer to restock the shelves!

You've told your mind and body you're going back to sleep. So your subconscious assumes it has another 90 minutes, but when the alarm goes off again after 10 or 15 minutes, your brain gets really confused. That's why you have foggy brain, which is technically called sleep inertia. And when this happens, it can take up to *four hours* for you to clear your mind and function at your best.

So if you have a habit of hitting the snooze button, I challenge you to tackle that habit right now. Just one hit and you've sabotaged your ability to start your day with an optimal mindset. You'll feel tired and out of sorts. Feelings of anxiety, fear, and uncertainty will quickly creep in. And if you're the least bit depressed, you've just made it worse.

It's so important in stressful and uncertain times that we take care of ourselves and each other. Accept what you can't control and focus on what you can. You can make small changes in your habits—like getting out of bed when the alarm goes off and not sleeping with your phone—that will give you a sense of control. Even small changes will give you a more positive mindset.

Last but not least, don't forget to take time away from your day job to have some downtime, some fun. I used to work with people who thought they couldn't take time off because the place where they worked would crumble if they weren't there. Seriously? Organizations evolve. Employees come and go. Everyone survives and life goes on.

Thinking that everything will fall apart if you take time off to rejuvenate is unhealthy, a bit silly, and also slightly arrogant. Yes, they will miss you, because undoubtedly you are a fantabulous person. But the world as you know it will still go on, even if you're not front and center.

Here's the thing, and why I put this in the section on physical and mental health: If you don't take time off to reflect and replenish, your body will tell you enough is enough and it will *make* you take time off.

Look around you. I'll bet you can spot the coworkers who are totally stressed out. It's only a matter of time until their bodies lay down the sick gauntlet so they are forced to take time for themselves and their health.

Okay, if you're thinking you'll just take the chance because your workplace simply can't go on without you, I get it. I used to be stuck in that same delusional world that was filled with people who just couldn't seem to tell the difference between reality and what they imagined was real.

Yes, at one time, I was that person. I went on vacations only because my husband wanted to go. I took my phone and usually my computer. I even braved a cybercafé in China, which was a surreal experience. You had to leave your passport at the door and have an employee sit with you while you used one of their computers. I felt like I was in some sort of spy movie and any minute the police would come busting in brandishing guns, gather up all the passports, and haul all the innocent people who couldn't take time away from cyberspace to god knows where.

But after our China trip, I figured it out. I was missing out on a lot by not leaving my job behind where it should have been left. I missed out on peaceful walks on beautiful beaches. I missed out on quality time with myself, my family, and my friends. And you know what? Every time I came back from a vacation, my job and the workplace were still there, just as I had left them. The world had carried on. Even without me to make sure it did. What a revelation!

And you know what's even better? My workplace is *still* alive and well without me. Yours will be okay too. They'll miss you, but the show will go on. Don't get me wrong—there's nothing wrong with working hard. But in today's world, keeping our phones glued to our hands and ears means that our brains are in constant overdrive. We don't take time to destress, and that can take a toll on our mental and physical health. Our brains need downtime to replenish and recharge.

So I ask you to try this on for size: Disconnect from your workplace. Leave it all behind, including the deadlines, workplace politics, and stress. Connect with those who mean the most to you in life, including yourself. Carving out periods where you detach your mind from work completely gives your brain the downtime it needs so you can come back refreshed.

Do the things that truly inspire you and that you love to do. Because really, what's the point of living if you're not doing it with passion and purpose and going all out?

And who knows—you might have serious breakthroughs or solve problems that seemed unsolvable before. Remember, you're not letting anyone down by valuing your mental health and taking time to protect it. Striking a healthy work/life balance is imperative for mental well-being and managing stress and depression, which can wreak havoc on an otherwise healthy body.

Be kind to your mind and body. They are the only ones you get in life.

While you're at it, live your life now. Don't wait until retirement.

Also remember that taking care of your health includes preventative measures. My husband gets a flu shot every year. I never do. Neither one of us has had a case of the flu in years. Go figure. Maybe it's genetics. I believe if you take care of your immune system, you go a long way toward fighting off illnesses, or as I like to say to my canine family member, a case of the "bad feels."

Around 80% of the immune system is situated in the digestive system. Your immune system is your friend, and it's more powerful than you might imagine. It creates, stores, and distributes the white blood cells that fight bacteria and viruses and protect your body from infection. To reduce stress and boost your immune system, be sure to:

- Eat adequate amounts of vitamin- and mineral-rich fresh fruits and vegetables.
- Get enough sleep.
- Exercise at low to moderate levels.
- Maintain a positive attitude.

If you can bolster the immunity scale of your gut, you are 70% of the way to fighting off viruses.

Give your full support to your mind and body health and, as with any friend, there will be perks. Choose to live your life by design, with passion and purpose. Make time to be inspired and have fun. Your body and your mind will thank you. So will the woman you're looking at in the mirror.

Chapter 16 Exercise

1. What one habit will you change that will result in better physical health?

   a. Exercise

   b. More restful sleep

   c. Better diet

2. What one habit will you change that will result in better mental health?

   a. Disconnect from your workplace

   b. Limit time on social media

   c. Other

Now that you know how to nurture and optimize your mental and physical health, it's time to think about your emotional well-being.

Chapter 17
Size Up Your Emotions ‖

"Anxiety is the great modern plague."

— Dr. Smiley Blanton,
American physician, psychiatrist,
psychoanalyst, and writer

*C*lose your eyes. Take a deep breath. How do you feel? Tired, emotionally drained, or full of energy?

That simple exercise will tell you a lot about your emotional health, which is just another term for how you feel. You see, many people focus on the mind and body, but neglect or just plain ignore their emotions. But if your emotional health is suffering, you can bet your mental and physical health are too.

Many factors contribute to your emotional health including:

- Genetics
- Overall mental and physical health
- Exposure to sunlight
- Thoughts (including that trash your ego sends your way)
- Life experiences
- Relationships you have with others

165

Fear, anxiety, and worry are unhealthy, destructive mental habits that can lead to serious health issues if left unchecked. The more you understand and are able to control your emotions, the more you can enjoy life, cope with stress, and focus on what's important.

You know, that life you dreamed and designed. The one you'll be living soon.

Unfortunately, most of us get so wrapped up in what's going on at the moment (and it's usually what's going *wrong* at the moment) that we miss out on all the awesomeness happening around us. Research has shown that different threats push unique psychological buttons. Hyperbolic media coverage—especially in this age where modern communication allows people to have a more intimate experience with threats like epidemics, terrorist attacks, and other extreme events—tends to exacerbate the situation. I know this because I worked in this world of communications.

Here's the thing: The media can be helpful when they are spreading accurate and useful information. Unfortunately, the industry has the propensity to find—and publicize—the worst. Why? Because that's what keeps you glued to your news source of preference, that's what boosts ratings, and that's what sells advertising.

It's about money. And if you're absorbing the news like a sponge during uncertain times, stop and think about what that big bowl of fear, anxiety, and worry they've set in front of you is doing to your emotional health. You're once again sucked into that low vibration that comes along with all that negativity, and that's not where you want to be.

Don't get me wrong: Fear is a natural human instinct designed to protect us in the moment, for the sake of survival. Its job is to always be on the lookout for what's wrong so you can fight, flee, or freeze when you're threatened. You also need to know what's going on in the world. My point is that you should be aware of the events and circumstances in your life, even if they might make you afraid. But you must learn to sift through all the information that comes your way—especially during uncertain, difficult, or fearful times—so you can reel yourself back in, sort through the emotion, process it, and make thoughtful decisions that are rational and reasonable based on your personal situation and what's right for you.

This helps you practice faith over fear. Faith is knowing in your core that you can handle whatever life throws your way, which makes it so much more powerful than any emotion, including fear. Replacing fear with the belief that you can handle any curve ball life throws at you will optimize your overall health and well-being.

Earlier, I talked about ridding yourself of the limiting subconscious beliefs that have been holding you back and kicking that big loudmouth ego to the curb to sprint outside your comfort zone. If you haven't done that, you're still stuck in your old life with your old habits. And that is affecting your emotional health. Instead of feeling good, you're still feeling bad, worrying, and coming from a place of self-doubt. You still haven't found your juju—your magic. You're still wishing and hoping for change.

Your true self wants to break out of the jail your ego has it in. To do that, you'll need to introduce your inner self to your source energy, and you'll need to connect the two often. Sometimes multiple times a day. You'll need to trust your inner guidance system to align itself with what you truly desire to find purpose, passion, and joy.

When you're feeling like shit, you're in a low vibrational state. Your emotional self is telling you that you're a little offtrack. That's okay. It's just time for an adjustment. Getting off-track is essential to your growth. Those negative emotions are opportunities to gain insight into where you are on your path.

So pause, take a deep breath or two, connect with your source energy, pivot if you have to, and you'll soon be back on the right path.

Here are a few ways you can do that. First, if you find you just can't stop worrying, practice emptying your mind at night. Take all your worries and place them one by one in a box. You can envision an imaginary box or use a real one, with slips of paper representing each worry. When you have them all tucked inside, shut the lid. Put it on your nightstand, or hand it over to God or your source. The day is done, so there's no sense worrying at this point. You can't change anything. So close the "worry box" and fill your mind with faith and peace.

I suggest you do this every night before going to sleep. The conscious mind tends to hang on to the last thoughts you have before you drift off to sleep. At that point, it is handing those thoughts off to your subconscious to file away in your mind's library while you're sleeping. You don't want the subconscious mind to file away all your worries and fears. Save the shelf space for something better like your dreams and aspirations— the fun stuff.

Finally, sometimes it's necessary to quiet all the noise in your head and all around you so your inner voice has a chance to be heard.

You may have to disconnect from social media, put down your phone or tablet, or unplug your television for a while. Especially if you're addicted to it or if it is causing you to be fearful and full of stress and anxiety. Try disconnecting for at least 30 minutes before you retire for the evening. It will give you a break from the day's mental stimulation and help you transition to a state of calm so you can sleep better. You'll survive—I promise.

It's impossible to make our thoughts disappear, and often the more we try to suppress them, the louder they become. But another way to tame them is to practice meditation.

Meditation is a great way to listen to your inner self and also to connect to your source energy. It's really just about practicing mindfulness. It's a mental training exercise for improving your awareness and your ability to pay attention to what's going on in your life. Meditation helps you build the skills you need to manage your stress, reduce negative emotions, increase imagination and creativity, gain new perspectives, and increase your self-awareness.

Most importantly, meditation helps you focus on the present instead of the regrets of the past or concerns about the future. You know, the things your ego likes to keep you focused on. The past can't be changed, so just move on. And the future isn't here yet. So if you're planning for tomorrow, that's okay. But worrying about things that haven't happened yet and may never happen is just plain silly and a waste of time.

For me, meditation consists of a daily devotional, quiet time, and sometimes yoga. But you may prefer guided meditation, energy clearing, walking in nature, or anything else where you are mindful of where and who you are in the present moment. Some runners get into a meditative state when they are running long distances. The act of moving puts you into the present moment and helps drown out the noise. When you connect with nature or with your inner self, you lose the obsessive focus on all the negative swirling around in this world. You refocus your mind.

There's no one right way, but a common practice is to focus on your breathing, on a word or phrase, or on a single point of reference. While you meditate, you pay attention to how your breath is moving in and out of your body. Breathe in positive thoughts and peace through your nose and exhale the negative vibrations through your mouth. Let them go. Shut off your thoughts and feel that connection to your source energy.

Regardless of how you do it, this practice is a key element in clearing away the clutter in your mind, reducing stress, relaxing, promoting an overall feeling of peace and happiness, and improving your emotional well-being.

Meditation has been practiced for thousands of years. It was originally meant to help deepen one's understanding of the mystical forces of life. Nowadays, it is used more to connect with our inner selves.

In an interview with Abbie Boudreau of *Good Morning America*, Goldie Hawn revealed her secret to happiness. She said that she started meditating in the 1970s to manage her panic attacks, and that meditation was a way to create a mindful sense of self so she could make better decisions. When Boudreau asked her how she found happiness, Hawn replied, "It isn't about finding happiness; it's about staying mindful about what makes you happy and those are two different things."

I also need a little extra help in connecting with my inner self and being mindful about a lot of things, including happiness. That's where meditation comes in. You might consider giving it a go and see if it will help you live each day practicing faith over fear and being happy. Your body and mind will thank you for it.

Chapter 17 Exercise

1. What one habit will you change to improve your emotional health?
    a. Will you quiet the noise by taking a break from hyperbolic media coverage and social media?
    b. Will you practice faith over fear?
    c. Will you hand over your "worry box" before you turn out the lights at night?
    d. Will you find time to meditate?
2. Write down your commitment to yourself.

You might be wondering how you can keep track of everything you're learning and doing on this new chapter journey. In the next chapter, you'll learn how keeping a journal can help.

Chapter 18
Keep A Journal ‖

A few years ago, I didn't quite get why anyone would waste time writing in a journal. I kept travel and work journals, but for some reason I never really thought about keeping a personal one.

Now I get it.

My travel journals in particular helped me understand the value in writing down my thoughts. All of them.

Journaling creates a written record of your life's journey—the ups, downs, and most notable events. It's a way of organizing your thoughts so you can process information and emotions more effectively, interpret your experiences, explore options, and make sense of stressful situations and challenges.

Processing your thoughts in this way helps you stay focused, reduces anxiety and stress, and improves your outlook on life. Journaling will help you stay in a positive vibration, which boosts your immune system and helps you sleep better.

It can also help you remember all the good things—the ups—that you've had so you don't get bogged down with negative juju when times are hard.

When I'm feeling low, my travel journals are a source of entertainment and flashbacks to happier times. They remind me about a once-in-a-lifetime trip to Vietnam where we toured from Hanoi to Ho Chi Minh City (formerly Saigon) with our dear friends and neighbors who had immigrated from Vietnam after Huê fell during the Tet Offensive. Touring Vietnam, meeting their friends and family members, and seeing the country through their eyes was extraordinarily special.

We've traveled to the Caribbean numerous times, and while we've visited a number of islands, we always spend some time in Barbados since that's where my husband and I met. I have captured many fond memories in my journals, but perhaps the most memorable was the time I ended up in the medical tent after nearly passing out at a World Cup cricket match. Yes, I had used sunscreen, had a hat on, and had been drinking water. But it was really hot. Still, it was rather embarrassing.

My other journals have French phrases written by a waiter in Martinique along with descriptions of various French dance styles and unique moves. Another journal described how I successfully convinced a busload of tourists to take a side trip to see a hydropower facility in Tahiti. No one was really interested except me, but they went anyway.

My European vacation journal is full of adventures from two Americans and three Scots touring the Italian countryside, sketches of various stone carvings in Pompeii, a delightful tour of Florence, and a description of my husband and an Italian woman negotiating the price for a room—in two different languages and by scribbling down and crossing out prices on a piece of paper.

We captured a lot of our experience on camera, but I also wrote about it in my journal because there was no other way to explain what was really happening. If you don't document your adventures in some way other than just pictures, I highly recommend it. Your words can be highly entertaining long after you return to your normal routine. I rarely look at my pictures, but I quite often read through my journals as a reminder of all the great adventures I've had and all I have to be grateful for.

Some people journal with the idea that they will pass their most intimate thoughts on to their children or grandchildren. It's a little like leaving your legacy as you define it rather than how others might remember it.

I wish my mother had done that. I'd like to know why my father loved to watch Louisiana State University college football. To my knowledge, we had no connection to Louisiana and I know for sure he didn't go to college there. Maybe he liked the color of the uniforms? Or the coach at the time? We'll never know. Mom could have cleared it up for us. Or if I had been a little smarter at the time, I could have asked the right questions and written the answers down in my own journal.

She also could have stored all her poems in a journal. She was never published, but every year she would write a poem and put it in our Christmas cards. I guess you could say she wrote and published for us. Regretfully, I only have a couple of them tucked away, but it sure would have been nice to have them all captured in her handwritten journal.

While it's not a journal, I do have her Bible, which has her favorite verses underlined and her notes and thoughts in the margin. It means so much when my daily devotional takes me to one of her favorites. Mom's poems and thoughts scattered throughout her Bible were her ways of processing her emotions and staying positive, even when times were tough. So I guess in a way, she was journaling. She just didn't know she was doing it.

Your journals and thoughts will be treasured by your loved ones long after you're gone.

During my corporate life, I wrote in my work journal every day. It's where I kept meeting and project management notes, ideas for improving policies and procedures, and customer and employee interactions and documentation. I kept them for years and referred to them often. They were particularly handy in keeping projects on schedule, recognizing milestones, and keeping my team focused.

Then during a major life transition a couple of years ago, I started keeping a personal journal. It shows me in black and white what's going on in my life and how I'm feeling about it. It can instantly help me sort through problems and helps identify my negative vibrations so I can sort them out, process the emotions, and get myself back into a high positive vibration. It helps me get out of my own damn way so I can see more clearly. I often look through it to remind me how far I've come and what I have to be grateful for.

Journaling can reveal times you're asking the Universe for more of what you *don't* want, based on those limiting beliefs your ego keeps throwing at you. When you read your negative thoughts, you can easily turn them around to positive ones and focus on what you *do* want in life.

Ultimately, it's a bit like writing your life's story. It can reveal areas where you are on track and also where you're getting out of sync with what you've designed for your future. Once you identify potential areas where you might get offtrack, you can figure out what you need to do to pivot or adjust. You already have a plan for your next chapter. But things change, that's life. It's how you manage that change that counts. When something unexpected happens or a new opportunity presents itself, journaling helps you sort through the emotion and figure out how it fits with your plan. It's like a pro/con exercise on steroids.

Journaling will also help you handle the curve balls life will throw your way. I know I've had my share and I'm sure you have too. You've got a plan, you're on a path, then out of the blue—WHAM. Something totally unplanned, and usually unwanted, happens.

I used to get stressed out. Well, sometimes it was a full-blown panic attack with blood pressure readings off the charts. On one occasion, thinking I was having a heart attack or stroke, my husband loaded me into the pickup and we headed for Urgent Care. One nurse said I had won the prize for the highest blood pressure that day. Great. Lucky me. Another one told me to go to my happy place, to which I replied, "I don't have one right now."

But I vowed never to let that happen to me again. I've been put to the test many times, but one event in particular made me realize how far I'd come and how the strategies I had adopted, including journaling, were working.

I call it assessing and adjusting, but it's just another term for a rational decision-making process. When faced with any situation, first make an assessment. Then identify and explore options. Consider the consequences—the risks and opportunities. Excessive risks may cause you to eliminate an option, and opportunities may cause you to reconsider an option you had overlooked or rejected. Evaluate your options against needs versus wants to determine their importance. Once you've finished the assessment, make a decision and adjust your path accordingly.

I had been really looking forward to a trip to Nashville for a training session and was disappointed because a terrible thunderstorm was about to descend on the airport. I'm not real comfortable in thunderstorms and am truly uncomfortable when I'm in an airplane in the middle of one.

The first thing I did was to let go of the idea I could control the weather, because I know I can't! I went for a walk (actually several) to clear my mind. I considered my options and evaluated my risks and opportunities.

Could I get a refund on my airline ticket? Yes.

Could I participate remotely? Yes.

Did I want to go? Yes, because I wanted to be with friends I hadn't seen in a while and wanted to experience the training with them.

Did I need to go? No. I wrote all my thoughts and emotions in my journal.

When you write your thoughts down and reflect on them, you are better equipped to deliberate and make a rational decision. Writing it down puts it in perspective.

Then I connected with my gut. What do I mean by that? Neuroscientists call intuition "emotional tagging," which means that each night, our brains store emotional responses to each experience or situation we encounter. When faced with a new decision, our brain goes into the library of past experiences and looks for similar experiences or patterns. Those manifest as our "gut" reaction or intuition. It's important to go through the assessment and analysis phase (the rational decision-making process), but also consider your instinct's insight and perspective. Journaling helps you connect with your gut.

Finally, I asked God for guidance, made a decision, cancelled my reservations, and put the opportunity wheels into motion. As soon as I did, I was immediately at peace.

Journal about what's happening, especially when things seem to be chaotic. When things get out of control in my life—or I feel like they are—I haven't always handled it well. I've been called a "control freak." But journaling helps me keep the control freak at bay. And after I'm done writing about it, I let it go. That's paramount.

I use my journals to get clarity, and more. As part of my morning routine, I like to write down what I'm grateful for, big or small. I always make sure I'm thriving on gratitude. There's nothing that will get you through the tough times like recognizing and being grateful for what has gone right and what you have in your life. By practicing gratitude, your attention is directed toward the positive aspects of your life instead of the negative.

Gratitude is a state of being. When you are in that state, you are raising your energetic vibration and when you do that, remember you are more connected with and aligned with your source energy. When you are ungrateful, whiny, disappointed, or angry, you are in a lower vibrational state, less connected and aligned with your source, and in a less powerful position to attract goodness into your life.

Grateful people are able to bounce back and recover quickly from setbacks or stressful situations. As a result, they are less likely to let bad events pull them into a downward spiral and more likely to grow in difficult times. In other words, gratitude makes us resilient. And resilience helps reduce stress and improves mental, emotional, and physical health. You'll even sleep more soundly. I promise.

Gratitude strengthens faith, which in turn smothers your fear of the unknown. Faith allows you to take risks, blast outside your comfort zone, and believe that the net will appear when you leap.

I practice gratitude now, but I wasn't always that way. It was easy to be grateful when things were going my way. But during the major life transition where my world seemed to be turned upside down, it was much harder to see anything good. Leaving my corporate career, selling my dream home, and living out of boxes for 10 months took its toll on my emotional, mental, and physical health. I lost my sense of purpose.

Let's face it. It's hard to be grateful for much of anything when you're feeling you've lost something...or everything.

But here's the thing: That's when you should be most appreciative.

I learned that even then I had a lot to be thankful for. I just needed to focus on that. Writing it all down in a journal helped me understand that I needed to embrace the change and look for the blessings. I know it sounds easy, and we all know it's not. But it truly is invaluable.

What did that look like? Well, we were living out of boxes, but we were staying with a family member and had the opportunity to spend precious time with her that we otherwise wouldn't have had. We have fond memories of our time spent together. Yes, I had sold my dream home, but in reality, it had become way too much for us and it was time to move on. Now I have a lovely home in a location closer to family and friends. We no longer have to spend a whole day driving in good and bad conditions to visit them. Yes, I had left my corporate career, but that opened up a whole new set of possibilities for me to live my next chapter by design, not default. I don't know why I waited so long.

As Tony Robbins once said, "When you are grateful, fear disappears and abundance appears."

So journaling can help you deal with change, find gratitude for the blessings in your life, ditch the fear of leaving your comfort zone, and replace it with faith that there's magic outside it. Faith drowns out your fear of the unknown. It allows you to take chances, to try something new. And when you do, your life will be filled with peace, love, and appreciation for all the good things that have come your way and awesomeness you are attracting into your world.

When you are in a constant state of gratitude and aware of all the splendor you have around you, you get over that lack mentality. You know there's more waiting for you, and it makes having faith that much easier. If you want to radically change your life and strengthen your faith that we live in an abundant Universe with plenty of everything to go around, be grateful for everything you now have and all the good that is hurtling toward you. Be grateful that you have the power to manifest any reality you desire, plan how you'll get there, and then leap into the unknown to go after it.

Life's too short for anything else.

Chapter 18 Exercise

If you haven't kept a journal in the past, will you commit to starting one today? Remember, your thoughts are extremely powerful. Journaling is a way you can stay in high vibration and a way for you to identify when you're asking the Universe for more of what you want and identify when you're getting offtrack. Journal about what's happening. Especially when things get out of control. And remember to practice gratitude in the good and hard times.

1. Write your first journal entry here or in the *Your Next Chapter* companion journal.

2. If you didn't purchase the companion journal, find a method or beautiful paper journal that works for you and just start.

3. Then make a habit of doing it every day.

Next you're going to learn some planning and time management tips to keep you organized and focused.

Chapter 19
Manage Your Time ‖

"If your habits don't line up
with your dream, then you need
to either change your habits
or change your dream."

— John C. Maxwell,
American author, speaker,
leadership guru, and pastor

*T*his chapter is about time management—how you're
going to plan your time to accomplish all you've set
out to do each day, week, month, and year.

No matter how organized you are, you still only get 24 hours
in a day. That doesn't change. So really, this chapter is about
how to manage *you* and what you do with the amount of time
you have.

If you struggle to fit everything into your day, you may need
to learn how to work smarter, not harder. You need to plan
and control how you spend your 24 hours to effectively work
your way through your action plan and accomplish your goals
and objectives. This will involve juggling your time between
your work and your personal life for a sustainable, stress-free
balance.

You've already established clear goals; now you must prioritize your actions so the ones that are truly important are at the top of the list and you can recognize and weed out the ones that perhaps shouldn't even be on the list. When you do this, you'll be better able to manage your time.

If you find that you're constantly scrolling through Facebook, Instagram, LinkedIn, or some other social media site, commit to breaking that time-consuming habit right now. Schedule social media time on your calendar. Set a timer for one hour or less. When your time is up, it's up. End of story.

You have to change your behavior and your habits—at least the ones that are sucking up all your time. So set time limits for tasks and stick to them.

A time management system can help. Use a paper calendar (my personal favorite), an electronic calendar, an app (MyLifeOrganized, Evernote, Todoist, or Toggl for example), or a napkin. Whatever works best for you. Even if it's a combination of methods.

One of the general managers I worked with claimed he used an electronic calendar. He did to some degree, so his administrative assistant could access it and help manage his appointments. But at the beginning of every week, he would print off the entire monthly calendar (and sometimes the following month or two) onto an 11" x 17" piece of paper, which he carried with him everywhere. Anytime you wanted to make an appointment or check availability with him, he would grin and say, "Just a minute. Let me pull out my electronic calendar," and he'd unfold his giant paper printout. Every. Single. Time. I just rolled my eyes. He's probably using the same "electronic" time management system today. But hey, it worked for him.

As you're scheduling your time, delegate any tasks you can to free your time up for the more significant ones. Ask for help. Hire a virtual assistant or figure out how you automate some processes if you need to. You'll be further ahead if you don't let less important tasks (or ones you're not that good at) derail your day.

I like to think I can do everything, but in reality, I can't. And in some cases, I shouldn't even try. Technology is a great example. Remember, I know just enough about it to be seriously dangerous. Thankfully, while in the corporate world, my roomful of computer wizards rescued me from the technology and cyberspace hell I often found myself in.

Recently, I upgraded my computer, and it was scary because there weren't any computer wizards at my disposal. I was flying solo.

The last time I tried to set up a new computer in my home office, it didn't go well. I couldn't get the cables, ports, or internet set up, my files wouldn't transfer, the security and antivirus settings were blocking some set-up functions, and I couldn't create a backup.

I was prepared for the worst, but this time everything seemed to be going so well. I took the computer out of the box and got it all set up. I turned it on and, like magic, it started walking me through the steps to transfer applications and data from my laptop to my new desktop. Easy peasy.

Then it happened. Almost everything I had stored in the cloud wouldn't sync. No matter what I did. I tried everything. Read through the online manual, tried a restart (or two or three). I could see my photos and files on my laptop, but nothing I did made them show up on my new desktop. My husband was just waiting for the meltdown to start. (In the past, I got so upset that neither he nor the Bouviers would come near.) I was close to tears but determined to figure it out.

I started to freak out, my blood pressure started to rise, and I could feel the tears starting to form. But then I took a deep breath, calmly printed off a couple of documents that I didn't want to get lost in cyberspace, and just shut everything down. In my best Scarlett O'Hara southern drawl I said, "I'll think about that tomorrow. Tomorrow is another day." Didn't give it another thought until the next morning.

That day, I tried to get the files to sync again and the results were the same. But here's the difference when you let go of old habits that haven't really served you well (like being stubborn and trying to do everything yourself) and put yourself in the right mindset.

I know my technology limitations, and I own them. I know I'm just not wired that way. It's not a character flaw, and it doesn't make me less of a person. So it was time to ask for help from a different roomful of wizards. It's called support, and it's there for many reasons, one of which is to keep users like me from jumping off the proverbial cyberspace cliff, having a panic attack, or seriously messing up a brand-new computer.

My support guy was amazing. But he had to consult with at least four other experts, including one "super expert" before my problem was resolved over an hour later. Five experts working on my technical issue for over an hour. I didn't feel so inadequate anymore. Especially when most of the trouble-shooting ideas were things I had already tried. But I'm grateful he stuck with me for that hour and that things turned out okay.

I asked for help rather than let it derail my day. That's effective time management.

So what kind of time management planning do I use? Glad you asked.

Every Sunday afternoon, I have an appointment with myself to plan the week, because I want to ensure I've accomplished key tasks before the end of the week.

What about you? Do you ever reach the end of the week and wonder where it went? Poof! Flew by! Gone! You made a to-do list. You had good intentions. But at the end of the week, many of the items are still on your list, still waiting for you to get it in gear and get them crossed off.

I used to have a lot of weeks like this. And it was a real downer. My Sunday afternoon planning appointment makes all the difference!

The first thing I do is review my goals—both personal and professional—because I want to be sure the activities I have planned for the week support them. If they don't, then they don't get "priority status." This is one way to keep focused on what really matters so I don't end the week with my high-priority items still on the list and my social media scrolling...well, taking priority.

Then I transfer the activities and appointments I've penciled in on my monthly calendar for the upcoming week to my weekly calendar, making sure to label them accordingly with colored pencils, like pink for personal activities, teal for personal development, and green for income-producing activities. As I'm transferring from my monthly to weekly calendar, I think about specific tasks that might need to be done in preparation for the event and jot these tasks down on the weekly calendar as well.

Next, I take a good, hard look at my week. I block out a realistic amount of time for each activity and note the time I'll shut things down for the day. I really enjoy my work, but since I work from home, I can get totally wrapped up in a project and forget all about the time and importance of maintaining a good balance between work and personal life.

But really, isn't that a good place to be in? I mean, I'd rather be writing down the time I'll stop working every day instead of watching the minutes slowly tick away until I can walk out the office door to the parking lot.

So now I'm ready for my week. And it will be productive because I've already made sure my activities are aligned with my goals (both personal and professional) and my week is packed with activities that I've deemed "priority status."

Be sure the tasks you put on your calendar are clearly aligned with all the work you did in Section II to design your next chapter. You know—your vision, goals, objectives, and action plan. If you've had to pivot, that's okay. Just make sure you've done so after much thought and that you've reflected it in your overall plan. No surprises!

While you must be realistic about your planning, scheduling, and effective time management, you must also acknowledge that you're going to have "down days" for whatever reason. Because let's face it—shit happens. Let that be okay. Just don't let it be every day.

Everyone has a down day. You know, the ones where you're not really feeling sad or depressed, you just can't get focused on what you had planned for that day. You've got it on your calendar but just can't get motivated. You're distracted. Your entire day is about to get derailed.

I had one recently. We took our puppy, Alli, for her morning walk. But when I settled in to my morning mindset routine with my cup of coffee, everything seemed "off." I just couldn't concentrate.

I could play the blame game. Blame the new home construction that had started on the lot next to us and right outside my office window. Blame the neighbors who called to let me know that construction had started (in case I couldn't see and hear the heavy equipment right outside my window). Blame my husband for interrupting my thoughts to give me a blow-by-blow. Blame my sister for dialing me up on FaceTime.

It was a morning filled with distractions. My ability to concentrate on anything I had on my calendar for the day was doomed. I definitely lacked focus and momentum. All my time management skills flew right out the window.

Here's how bad it got: I started working on our income taxes. That is a surefire way to set my mood. Trust me, it's not a good mood either. I had allowed all the distractions to derail my day.

But the next day was a time for reflection. Just about everything I thought had gone wrong, in reality, was a lesson in what had actually gone right.

I took another walk to clear my head. We had already taken Alli for a walk that day as part of my morning routine, but getting in the right mindset doesn't just happen first thing in the morning. It's important to pay attention to it throughout the day and adjust when you need to. Instead of trying to control every minute of every day, I try to spend time—in the moment—to reflect on what is happening and why.

I was able to avoid the blame game because I've learned that it's not productive, it allows me to stay in a negative vibration, and I often miss the blessings coming my way. The new home construction work? We knew it would happen this year, so why was it a surprise? After living on 12 acres and feeling rather isolated, we're thankful we have neighbors and that we live among interesting, awesome people who are also friends.

Those friends (neighbors) who called to tell me about the construction? They didn't want us to be surprised and wanted to get together one last time before there was a house in between us.

And when my husband gave me a blow-by-blow, I should have thought about how thankful I am that he's in my life and that we have an opportunity to talk about what's going on in the moment instead of at the end of a draining workday.

This is how gratitude can put you back on the positive vibration track.

My sister's FaceTime call was the biggest lesson of the day. She runs a highly successful kitchen and bath business and is also a computer programmer. We started talking about tax programs, and she suggested a few ways I could be more organized so I wasn't so frantic when tax season rolled around. She's younger but often wiser. Our conversation put me light years ahead in managing next year's tax season.

Flexibility is so important when planning and managing time. Sometimes the distractions are God's way of guiding me in a certain direction, even though it's often hard for me to recognize that when I'm in the moment. But I'm getting better. (I'm a work in progress too.)

At the end of every 30 days, I take time to reflect on the past month and plan for the new one. I review my goals and action plan and ask myself whether I'm happy with how I spent my time. If not, I write down the steps I'll take the next month to adjust and improve.

I write about my achievements right after they happen and include enough detail to learn from them. Especially if I want to make them happen again! At the end of the month, I also review my accomplishments and celebrate all the things I'm proud of. I pick out the one thing I was especially grateful for the past month. I write down three things I can improve on during the next month and, if I don't already have those included in my action plan, I outline concrete actions I'll take to work toward these improvements.

Finally, I do a major review and planning session at the end of every year. Most people plan their new year by making resolutions. I used to do the same but not anymore, because I've watched so many people make resolutions year after year that just fall by the wayside. In fact, statistics indicate only 64%

of these goals last longer than the first month, and only 46% last longer than six months. That just sets people up for disappointment. And that's exactly how I used to feel.

Like many, I used to start out the year with such good intentions. Lose weight. Get in shape. Get a new job. Clean out the closets, declutter, and reorganize. (I have to be desperate to do that!)

But then those resolutions just faded away. And when that happened, I felt terrible. Stressed out. Disappointed. So it got me thinking. Since I'm all about having the right mindset to live life by design, why not ditch the tired and clichéd New Year's resolutions that just don't stick and make a decision—a commitment—to myself.

Resolutions fade; commitments live on.

As renowned success mentor Darren Hardy said, "Commitment is doing the thing you said you were going to do long after the mood you said it in has left you."

Your commitments should be based on your vision, values, goals, and objectives. See? All the work you did to design your next chapter is the foundation for turning that into your reality. It all fits together perfectly.

So here are five things you can do to plan for a productive and profitable new year.

First, spend some time reviewing the prior year. It's a great way to remind yourself of personal and business events and accomplishments. You'll find that sometimes the big events (whether good or bad) drown out the things you've done every day to move you closer to your dreams and goals. But in the end, even those baby steps are important. Reflecting on your accomplishments—big and small—is a great way to shift your mindset from one of regrets or scarcity to one of abundance!

After you review your year, ask yourself some questions. Write down the best thing that happened. There's always something that makes the year unforgettable. No year is perfect, but I can guarantee that you did have wins and that's where you need to focus to stay in a high, positive vibration.

Write down what you enjoyed doing the past year, because you'll definitely want to take that into your next one. Write down the messages in your mess, because these identify your learning experiences and circumstances where you were most likely pushing past your fears and moving outside your comfort zone. Write down how you changed or evolved and where you found the magic. Then pat yourself on the back.

For the next year, focus on your intention rather than the outcome. The result you want is to achieve your goal, but your intentions are based on what's happening in the moment and are instrumental in influencing the actions you'll take to move you closer to your goal. This is crucial because focusing on the end result (which is usually a large project) can often be overwhelming and it takes time. If you're like most people, you'll quickly grow impatient. Your ego will kick in and try to tell you you're not making any progress—or worse, that you should give up because you're never going to get there. Then all of a sudden, you're part of that 64% that has ditched a resolution in the first month.

Instead, think about exactly how you intend to achieve your goals. Break them down into manageable "bites" and make each one an intentional step you'll take on your journey to your destination.

For example, one of my goals was to write a book, and I had to break it down into reasonable, attainable steps to keep myself on track and moving in the right direction. Those steps, my intention, were to:

- Schedule time on my calendar every day to write at least 1,000 words.
- Read through the first draft and mark sections to research and review.
- Conduct additional research.

- Hire an editor.
- Hire a book cover graphic designer.
- Schedule time to revise the manuscript.
- Research publishing options.

These intentions kept me focused on what I needed to do every day to move me closer to my goal without getting bogged down in negative self-talk or overwhelmed.

If your goal is tied more closely to a lifestyle change than completing a project, your intention should be to create new habits. Weight loss is a great example. Nearly two-thirds of adults and one-third of children and adolescents in the United States are overweight or considered obese. About 45% of those overweight and 67% of those who are obese are trying to lose weight, with 15% of those adults spending about $2.1 billion a year on weight-loss supplements alone.

Yet medical professionals and health experts advise that making lifestyle changes such as adopting healthy overall habits that manage weight and promote overall health are better long-term solutions than fad diets and supplements that offer temporary, short-term outcomes for weight loss.

So if one of your goals is to lose 10 or 20 pounds in six months (and keep it off), here's how you might break that down into manageable bite-sized pieces.

- Research healthy lifestyle plans designed to also help you lose weight.
- Pick the one that is within your budget and is a plan you can reasonably follow.
- Make weekly meal plans.
- Set up an exercise routine.
- Join a support group.
- Evaluate your progress every week.
- Celebrate your wins.

If you ask Google to tell you how long it takes to form a new habit, the answer will be anywhere from 21 days to establish one and up to 90 days to make it a lifestyle change. In a paper published in the European Journal of Social Psychology, Phillippa Lally contends it takes an average of 66 days to form a habit. But that varies depending on the type of habit and how hard it might be to sustain new behaviors. (Drinking an extra glass of water every day would be a much easier habit to create than running an hour a day when you don't like to exercise.)

Since you're pursuing lifestyle changes, you'll want to make sure your new habit is foolproof. My advice is to forget how many days it takes and just focus on your intentions (your journey) with your eye on the prize (your destination).

I can assure you it will be worth it.

Don't forget to journal, reflect, and celebrate. Your journal will not only help you stay focused on all you intend to accomplish, it will also document the progress you're making. When that old ego starts screaming, "It's taking too long!" or "It's time to give up," you have the proof to say otherwise.

So every year, plan how you're going to chase your dreams and turn them into reality. Then break them down into monthly, weekly, and daily goals. Schedule and use your time deliberately, but remember to stay flexible. Create habits that support your plan. And most of all, go easy on yourself even when you're having an occasional down day. You deserve it.

Chapter 19 Exercise

Take some time to plan out exactly how you will manage your time.

1. What type of time management system will you use?

2. How will you ensure you are working on the most critical tasks and nothing will be missed?

3. How and when will you evaluate your progress against established goals and objectives?

4. What habits do you need to change so your activities are aligned with the dream life you've designed?

Now it's time to take action.

Chapter 20
Take Action

"Comparison is the thief of joy."

— Theodore Roosevelt,
American president, statesman,
conservationist, naturalist, and writer

J'd add that comparison is also the thief of dreams.

Chances are you are creating a next chapter that is different from the one that is now your reality. Otherwise what's the point, right? You might have made a few tweaks here and there, or you may have designed a next chapter that turned into a major overhaul. As long as your design is based on your core values and you were honest and true to yourself, it doesn't matter.

Now the real work begins: You actually have to take action.

I know you're all gung ho right now, and that's good. I don't want you to lose that enthusiasm and excitement, ever. This is a journey and you just took the first step. You won't reach your destination tomorrow. You'll have good days and bad. You may have to go back and review sections of this book when the going gets tough and when you get discouraged. It happens to everyone.

While I was writing this book, I read a personal development book written by an extremely witty author. I made a huge mistake: I started comparing my work to hers. My ego was running amok trying everything to sabotage the whole project, telling me, "You're not good enough. No one will read your book. Why are you wasting your time?" I was definitely out of my own damn lane. In fact, I had completely crossed the center line. Thankfully, my business coach talked me off the ledge before she gave me a firm kick in the butt.

You see, sooner or later we all get caught in the comparison trap. It's hard not to do. Especially when it comes to social media where people tend to post about all the fabulous stuff going on in their lives, when of course they're only showing what they want others to see. But stop comparing yourself, your life, and your journey to others. When you do this, you are holding yourself back.

So you may have the same goal as someone else, but you may not be able to reach yours as quickly or easily as they did. You might have to take a class or two to gain the certifications you need in your next chapter. That doesn't mean that it's impossible; it just means you're different and you have some work to do.

If you aspire to be like someone else, that's okay! Just remember, everyone—including you—has to start somewhere. So just take the first step.

Steve Jobs was given away for adoption by his biological parents. He became interested in electronics after his foster dad showed him the joys of technical tinkering in their garage. He had to drop out of college because his education was costing his foster parents a lot. He returned Coke bottles to earn money and took free meals at the Hare Krishna temple. A hippie who used to trip on LSD (probably not something he was proud of), Jobs went from a technician in Atari to becoming the CEO of Apple (definitely something to be proud of).

And how could I not mention Oprah Winfrey, especially since she's the role model for just about every female entrepreneur out there. Oprah grew up in severe poverty in rural Mississippi. She suffered physical and sexual abuse. But she went on to work for a local radio station (a job that launched her passion for media), earned a scholarship to Tennessee State University, and became the first African American television correspondent in the state at the age of 19. She has launched numerous careers and now boasts a net worth of $3.2 billion.

The key is to not compare where you are now to where they are now. They started somewhere; success didn't happen overnight. But neither of these individuals listened to their ego or let limiting beliefs or fears stop them from achieving their dreams. They started. They failed. They kept going, following their heart with determination and grit.

So just start. Right where you are now. You have the power to create something just as magical, but your journey will be on your own terms and timeline. And in your own damn lane.

Remember, you are unique. You're influenced by outside forces and people, but the key is to absorb all that information and filter it according to your own belief system and your own values. The comparison game is the ego's demand to be the best. Not everyone is cut out to be the leader of the pack or be in the spotlight. Many don't even desire this. So if it's not your desire to be a radio and television personality like Oprah, don't do it and don't beat yourself up over it. If it is your aspiration, go for it. Just make sure you're following your heart's desire, and not your ego's or anyone else's.

The ego wants instant gratification; it wants you to achieve your goals as quickly as possible. To be a concert pianist when you're just learning and practicing scales. To win a marathon when you can barely run a mile. Your ego wants you to live your dream NOW, when you haven't even made it to the end of the book yet let alone started your own journey.

This instant gratification is rooted in the need to win the approval of others. The only person that needs your approval is you.

The comparison game is one very convincing way your ego has of keeping you safely inside your comfort zone. But you've designed a next chapter that is full of magic, and it's likely outside that space. So go for it, because you deserve it.

I know from personal experience how easy this sounds and how difficult it can be. When I started my direct sales business, it was hard not to compare my beginning to someone else's success after seven or eight years of hard work.

Here are a few tips you can use to avoid falling into the comparison game trap. Catch yourself in the act of...

> ...comparing yourself to someone else. This requires awareness and, in some situations, taking action. If you find yourself feeling inferior every time you read posts from "that friend" who has such a perfect life, perhaps it's time you unfollowed or unfriended them. If you do this, you'll become a stronger, more positive, and more confident person.
> ...comparing your life journey to someone else's. Keep things in perspective. Comparing yourself to that person who is wildly successful in a business she started eight or ten years ago when you only started two years ago or last month isn't putting things in perspective. You don't know what sacrifices she made, the hours she clocked, or the failures she had. Let her work be a motivator for you, not competition. You can use it to identify goals you'd like to achieve, and as inspiration for your own life. Hell, you can even call her up and find out how she did it. Trust me, she will be honored you asked.
> ...allowing negative thoughts to leave you feeling like you have no options, that you're stuck where you are. In reality, it's not because you have no options

or can't do it, it's because you won't even try because of the self-imposed limitations.

...not practicing gratitude. Being grateful for who you are and acknowledging the talent you have will help you realize your options and potential.

I encourage you to inspire and motivate others. And be aware of ways other people's success stories are inspiring you as well.

But stay focused on you, and make your journey your own. Personal development, a commitment to lifelong learning, and adopting new behaviors, habits, and mindsets means you are constantly assessing and improving every area of your life. Working on creating the best version of yourself helps keep you out of the comparison game. You're less likely to allow the opinions of others to affect how you live or achieve your best life because you know you are already working to design and live it. Focusing on yourself leaves less time to get preoccupied with what's going on in the lives of others, less time for the comparison game.

Above all, love yourself.

Chapter 20 Exercise

What action steps will you take to make sure you avoid the comparison trap and stay in your own lane? Write them down in your journal and refer to them when you feel yourself getting discouraged.

One way you can stay focused and in action is to start your day off with a morning mindset routine, where all the work you've done so far will come together.

Chapter 21
Stage Your Day To
Slay Your Day ‖

T his is where it's all going to come together for you. I
promised you this would make sense at some point.
Now seems like the perfect time.

A couple of years ago, as I was in the thick of "unbecoming" a
person I really didn't like and revealing who I wanted to be in
my next chapter, I learned (and was reminded of) some things
I'd need to do to find the confident woman I had been before.
There were so many moving parts to my new puzzle called
daily life. I had so much flexibility and time freedom, but I
also had a lot to accomplish. This new journey was essential,
and each step on my path needed to be deliberate if I was going
to realize my dreams.

I'm not known for having a lot of patience. I tend to want things
immediately. But during a mastermind session, a really wise
business coach opened my eyes to the importance of enjoying the journey rather than just focusing on the destination.
Participants were asked to present three things: a major win,
a challenge, and a way the group could help. I was prepared.
Or so I thought.

I listened to several participants and wrote down my thoughts
and best advice based on the challenge and the ask they

presented. But when it was my turn to speak, I looked around the room and immediately got emotional. My win was easy. I had clarity on my business goals. Yeah! Then I looked at all the beautiful (young) women in the room, and with tears streaming down my face, these words came out:

"But things aren't moving as quickly as I want them to, and I'm afraid at my age I won't have enough time to accomplish everything I've set out to do."

I went on to present my challenge and asked my creative minds to help me come up with a "sexy" name for the online course I was designing.

The people in my mastermind had some ideas for my business challenge, but every single one of them started with something like "You are not old; you're just getting started. What an inspiration you are to others starting a new journey. The world needs you." As they were providing feedback, my business coach stood up, turned the chart around so we couldn't see it, and started drawing. When she turned it back around, we saw that she had drawn a beautiful forest in the middle with a stick figure of me on the left and my "destination" on the right. This is what she said:

> Christy, you are looking at it too linearly. I am here, I am trying to get there, and I will only be happy and fulfilled when I get there. The reality is that this forest—the journey—is the secret sauce, the magic, and the growth. It's like you are on a road trip to get to the beach and you have to drive through a magical forest, but because you're only focused on the beach, you are totally missing all the gifts that journey has put in front of you—just for you!

She was right. I was missing magic along the way because I was too focused on my ultimate prize—a successful online business. But how could I enjoy the journey without frustrating the impatient inner child who was throwing a tantrum because she thought time was running out?

I needed some method that would provide daily focus and clarity on the goals, objectives, and tasks I had in my action plan (my journey) but also remind me of the ultimate prize (my destination). That daily routine would ease my anxiety about running out of time and allow me to recognize and appreciate the gifts as they came my way.

I had read a couple of books about setting up a morning routine, and I developed one that suited my lifestyle and worked for me. I followed it most mornings. But now it was time to get serious. Jim Rohn said, "Either you run the day or the day runs you." It means you have to take charge and have a plan of action, or time just gets away from you and you won't be productive. I was ready to run my day.

The effort you've put forth to design your next chapter can now be rolled into a morning mindset routine that will help you run your day so your day doesn't run you.

But it really starts the night before. If you're anything like me, you have some old habits that are no longer serving you, which you'll need to get rid of and replace with ones more aligned with your new plan. Let's see if I'm right.

Let's say you want to implement a morning mindset routine but you have a habit of grabbing your phone before you're even out of bed. Next thing you know, you've been on social media or checking email or a newsfeed for half an hour. One thing leads to another, and the plans you had for the first hour or two in the morning are toast.

Getting swept up in what's going on in the world before you get into the right mindset to seize the day is a common habit that you can change. If you do, you'll be more focused and more productive. To change this habit, do four things every evening.

1. First, put your cell phone in a different room. Our phones have become our #1 distraction in life. They are the first thing we check in the morning and are rarely out of our sight (or hands) the rest of the day. A staggering 33% of us wake up in the middle of the night to check the phone! But no more (unless you have extenuating circumstances like a family emergency or a natural disaster looming). You're taking control of when you let the world in.
2. Then set your old-fashioned alarm clock for 30 minutes earlier than when you would normally wake up. If you don't have one, then set an alarm on your phone but put it on the other side of the room.
3. Next, write down three things you want to accomplish the following day. This will take away the urge to focus on making decisions as soon as you wake up, and it will free up energy and time for more productive activities.
4. Finally, place a pen and your journal (or plain old paper) in that empty space on your nightstand. You know, where your phone used to be. (You'll see why in a minute.)

The next morning when the alarm starts buzzing, you may be tempted to hit the snooze button. "Just give me ten more minutes," you moan. Instead, get up! But if you're tempted to race for your phone, stop yourself.

Instead, you now have a morning mindset routine, your brain's "cup of joe," waiting for you. You are worth 30 minutes to yourself before you let the world into your space.

As you're stretching, brushing your teeth, or taming your morning bedhead, think about the accomplishments you wrote down the night before. Let your mind mull over one step you could take to help you accomplish the goals. Give your mind the time and space without distractions, and let it shape the course of your day. Then write down what you plan to do and also why it matters. That pen and journal (or paper) you put where your phone used to be will come in handy.

Now you're ready for the activities that will put you in the right mindset to slay your day.

So what's my morning routine?

I start each morning by taking care of my physical health. As soon as I get up, I drink a 12-ounce glass of water to hydrate. I also drink warm water with lemon and honey. I read somewhere years ago that it keeps the body free from toxins and infectious bacteria, boosts immunity, helps with skin conditions such as acne, and replenishes energy.

Then it's off on a walk through the neighborhood, where my husband and I take in the beauty of the landscape, Discovery Bay, and the Strait of Juan de Fuca, and puppy Alli contemplates which birds or deer she will try to chase. (She has an incredible prey drive.) We talk to each other and with neighbors we encounter. Sometimes we just enjoy the silence, deep in our own thoughts.

This is usually my first time for daily gratitude. For my nice, comfortable home, physical health (ability to walk), emotional health (positive vibrations), and my family (including the furry, four-legged one) with me. I'm also thankful I'm able to enjoy life on my own terms in a beautiful setting.

After our walk, I write these down in my journal along with other thoughts I've had since I opened my eyes.

My breakfast is more than a cup of coffee with sugar on the go. I start my day with something nutritious that's good for my mind and body. I'm a leftover kind of gal, so it's either that or fruit and yogurt. And an occasional good ole American breakfast that includes eggs.

With my exercise and journaling checked off, I then spend about 10 minutes reading my daily devotionals to strengthen my relationship with my source energy and to put me at the highest vibrational energy and right mindset to tackle the rest of my day.

I review my personal and professional vision statements. I visualize myself at my final destination, as if my dreams are reality. Then I read through my goals and objectives to make sure I'm clear on where I'm going and how I'm going to get there.

Next I read through my affirmations. My list is fairly long, but yours doesn't have to be.

One of my affirmations is "I am focused and in action every day." And I am, thanks in large part to my morning mindset routine.

Another one is "I am bold, courageous, and confident." This one is important to me because when I left my corporate job, I became unsure about myself. I lacked confidence in my abilities. But I cared deeply about these qualities and wanted them back. They were nonnegotiable, and that's why I affirm the fact that they are a part of me every day.

I missed writing after leaving my corporate job, so one of my affirmations is "I am a brilliant and prolific writer." That is why I blog and one reason I wrote this book.

Words alone do not attract, but when you feel emotion as you speak your affirmations, your vibration is strong and you attract or manifest what you want. Spending a few minutes every day on these deliberate, powerful thoughts in combination with strong, positive emotion will attract circumstances and events into your life that you want. Daily affirmations are your way of declaring to the Universe what you want.

Finally, I take a look at my to-do list for the day, which is really my system for breaking goals down into manageable action items. I rely on my paper (yes, paper) planner, which has half-hour time slots starting at 6:00 am and ending at 10:30 pm with space to list personal and work tasks for the week. Each week, I block out time for appointments and action items. I'm flexible though, so when I do see something that needs to be done, I can figure out how to fit it in with the rest of what I have planned for that day and week.

It's a system that keeps me on track, putting one foot in front of the other, and moving forward deliberately and purposefully with the lowest number of distractions.

And there's beauty in doing it that way. When you break down your big, badass goals into smaller tasks and action items, you're really moving yourself closer and closer to your goals. And you will have done that without feeling overwhelmed, without procrastinating, and without quitting.

Then you'll be all set to get started with your day.

Try it. I think you'll be pleasantly surprised at how it sets the stage for a positive, productive day.

Chapter 21 Exercise

1. Think about how you start your day, from the time you wake up to when you leave for work or enter your home office.
2. Write down what you will do in each of the following areas:
   a. Physical health (include diet and exercise)
   b. Mental/emotional health
   c. Affirmations
   d. Self-improvement
   e. Vision, goals, and action plan
   f. Gratitude

Living Your Dream ‖

*I*f you're considering a change, now is an ideal time. You are shaping a new American dream that involves making a living doing what you love and stepping into a workday that was designed by you, aligned with your core values and dreams. It comes from a place of peace and joy. There's no need for you to feel stuck where you are, and it's the perfect time to design a new chapter you'll enjoy.

And now you also have the right mindset and the tools to make it happen!

The labor environment continues to evolve. Generational interests for the type of work desired and the demographics of the workforce in general are changing. New technologies and shifts in societal and customer demands are rapidly changing the business landscape. The eight-hour, structured workday is giving way to a gig economy and a world of young leaders, innovators, entrepreneurs, and creators—people who would rather live by their playbook than follow someone else's.

As of 2018, 36% of workers (approximately 57 million people) were part of the gig economy. That number is expected to rise as the 2020 financial crisis and unemployment rates (approaching half what it was during the Great Depression) cause workers to reinvent themselves. Businesses will also evolve as automation expands, labor practices and regulations are updated, and the desire for a more flexible workforce improves.

So if you're not content with "traditional" work options, just know there's a new world out there. You can without a doubt be part of it. And even though the school system still lags behind in teaching budding entrepreneurs the skills they need to be successful, plenty of other experienced mentors in this arena have your back.

It has already begun. If you've ever taken an Uber or Lyft, ordered food delivery from Grubhub, or rented a vacation home through Airbnb, you've supported our gig economy. In the US, this new trend has provided millions of people with an easy way to tap into the world of working independently, on their own terms.

Additionally, the rise in e-commerce platforms, decline of brick-and-mortar retail stores, and double-digit unemployment rates of 2020 mean more virtual opportunities than ever to sell products and services and freelance or work remotely from home. The rise of e-commerce means you no longer need to invest in renting commercial real estate and rely on local foot traffic; instead, you can market your products and services internationally.

In 2019, US online retail sales of physical goods amounted to $365.2 billion and are projected to reach close to $600 billion in 2024. I'll bet you've known a person or two who sold on Amazon, Etsy, or eBay, which are some of the most popular online stores as of 2020. You've probably bought from some of them as well.

And you probably know others who are involved in business models that depend on person-to-person sales by independent representatives who often work from and build a business from home. In fact, since 2015, global retail sales from direct selling increased from about $184 billion to approximately $192 billion in 2018.

E-commerce isn't for everyone. But if the next chapter you've designed put you squarely in the Creator Zone of Genius that you learned about in Chapter 7, one of your first goals should be to research options. I promise you there are excellent brands out there, and an individual with a lot of energy and good communication skills can create a profitable business with a modest investment.

Or if you just want a hobby or to make enough money in a side gig for a shameless shoe fund, direct sales may be your ticket. I've seen women succeed on all levels. The beauty is that it's entirely your decision and your success is up to you.

Our small-business economy thrives on freelancers with entrepreneurial spirits, hustle and drive, and professional skills. They—and we—are changing the traditional business model. This new one is quickly becoming the backbone of our country while continuing to grow. The 2010 Census reported 27.9 million small businesses registered in the United States. Of those, 52% were home-based, 36% were owned by women, and 73.2% were sole proprietors. In just eight short years, that figure rose to 30.2 million small businesses, roughly 60% of those home-based.

According to the *New York Times,* about 43% of the US workforce performed some work remotely in 2016, revealing the trend in organizations to become more flexible. According to the article, "Employees are pushing companies to break down the long-established structures and policies that traditionally have influenced their workdays." This rise of remote work and the growing comfort level of employers to hire independent contractors or let employees work from home is creating new opportunities for solopreneurs to start their own home-based businesses based on their specific set of skills.

Fast-forward to the 2020 global coronavirus pandemic, where we got a glimpse of how creative organizations and employees could be under government restrictions. Gallup, a global analytics and advice firm headquartered in Washington, DC, found that 62% of employed Americans worked from home during the crisis, and over half of those indicated they would prefer to continue working remotely as much as possible after restrictions are lifted. Managers surveyed tended to agree that the crisis would likely change remote work policies moving forward. Gallup predicts that greater remote work could become the next normal.

Bottom line is that if you have an interest in working from home, you can leverage your skills and expertise and turn that into a home-based business or redefine the office job you have today.

Time is going to pass whether you're working on your dreams or not. You have to do the things that scare you, that push you outside your comfort zone. That's how you'll prove to yourself that you are stronger and more powerful than you thought. You have made a decision, so now it's time to go for it.

Go all in. Do the work. Be consistent. Tackle your fear.

Remember that any burning desire or commitment of your heart will be met with resistance. Your ego will pitch a hissy fit. Don't settle for what it thinks is good enough or something someone else has said you should settle for, instead of what you truly want deep down in your soul and from the bottom of your heart.

Your ego doesn't want you to evolve; it wants to keep you right where you are. It feeds on your fears.

- Fear of being selfish.
- Fear of sacrificing your family's dreams for yours.
- Fear of throwing away the education, training, and preparation that those we love have sacrificed so much for and that we have worked so hard for.
- Fear of being ridiculed.
- Fear of stepping into the unknown.
- Fear of failure.

Don't listen to your ego's doubts and excuses! The world and workplace are constantly evolving. Why shouldn't you embrace the amazing opportunity to evolve and step into the life of your dreams?

Dig deep inside to your true self, where your dreams and ideas live. Turn every one of those fears into faith.

- Faith that a better workday will make you and your family happier and more fulfilled.
- Faith that your education, training, and preparation will serve you well in your newly designed workday.
- Faith in knowing that everyone fails, and what makes you stronger is how you handle it—what you learn and how you apply that to create an even bigger, brighter future.
- Faith that you'll find the magic...because you will.

I believe that each of us comes into this world with a specific destiny. We have a job to do. Figure out what that is and get to work. But when things aren't happening as quickly as you think they should, remember that divine timing is perfect timing. It will happen when it's meant to happen.

Show up for yourself every day, even if it's only for a half hour or so. This is a true commitment, not a New Year's resolution that will fall by the wayside.

So start today. There's no better time. Dream, design, and plan for the future but live in the moment and stay in your own damn lane.

I hope I've inspired you to take that leap of faith and go for it.

Life is an amazing journey—a story with chapters and pages that are unique to each of us. Each one matters. I'm looking forward to hearing all about yours.

References

Chapter 1

Davis, Nicholas. "5 Ways of understanding the Fourth Industrial Revolution." World Economic Forum. November 16, 2015. https://www.weforum.org/agenda/2015/11/5-ways-of-understanding-the-fourth-industrial-revolution/.

Gray, Alex. "The 10 skills you need to thrive in the Fourth Industrial Revolution." World Economic Forum. January 9, 2016. https://www.weforum.org/agenda/2016/01/the-10-skills-you-need-to-thrive-in-the-fourth-industrial-revolution/.

"Generational Differences in the Workplace." Infographic. Purdue University Global. https://www.purdueglobal.edu/education-partnerships/generational-workforce-differences-infographic/.

Chapter 2

Calao, J.J. "The Inside Story Of Snapchat: The World's Hottest App Or A $3 Billion Disappearing Act?" Forbes. January 6, 2014. https://www.forbes.com/sites/jjcolao/2014/01/06/the-inside-story-of-snapchat-the-worlds-hottest-app-or-a-3-billion-disappearing-act/.

"Vera Wang Bridal House Ltd." Encyclopedia.com. 2020. https://www.encyclopedia.com/people/literature-and-arts/fashion-biographies/vera-wang/.

Chapter 3

The King Center. https://thekingcenter.org/about-tkc/martin-luther-king-jr/.

Cameron, Julia. *The Artist's Way: A Spiritual Path to Higher Creativity.* Jeremy P. Tarcher/Putnam. March 4, 2002.

Cherry, Kendra. "The Role of the Conscious Mind." Verywell Mind. Updated June 1, 2020. https://www.verywellmind.com/what-is-the-conscious-mind-2794984/.

Ananthaswamy, Anil. "NeuroLogic: The enthralling story of the unconscious mind." New Scientist. February 10, 2016. https://www.newscientist.com/article/2076606-neurologic-the-enthralling-story-of-the-unconscious-mind/#ixzz6U5knquK5/.

McLeod, Saul. "Sigmund Freud's Theories." SimplyPsychology. Updated 2018. https://www.simplypsychology.org/Sigmund-Freud.html.

Solms, Mark. "What is 'the unconscious,' and where is it located in the brain? A neuropsychoanalytic perspective." PDF. New York Academy of Sciences. 2017. https://www.sas.upenn.edu/~cavitch/pdf-library/Solms_Unconscious.pdf.

Timbrell, Peter. "The Science." Roots to Branches. 2017. https://www.roots-to-branches.co.uk/the-science.

Galifianakis, Zach and Robert Downey, Jr. *Due Date.* DVD. Directed by Todd Phillips. Warner Bros. Pictures, 2010.

Chapter 4

"Hydropower." Northwest River Partners. https://nwriverpartners.org/hydropower/.

Form, William. "Social change." Encyclopaedia Britannica. Update November 16, 2020. https://www.britannica.com/topic/social-change.

Johns, Merida L. "Breaking the Glass Ceiling: Structural, Cultural, and Organizational Barriers Preventing Women from Achieving Senior and Executive Positions." Perspectives in Health Information Management. National Center for Biotechnology Information (NCBI). January 1, 2013. https://www.ncbi.nlm.nih.gov/pmc/articles/PMC3544145/#:~:text=The%20impenetrable%20barriers%20between%20women,Glass%20Ceiling%20Commission%20in%201995.&text=The%20commission%20also%20found%20that,that%20of%20their%20male%20counterparts/.

Lagerberg, Francesca and Kim Schmidt. "Women in Business 2020: Putting the Blueprint into action." PDF. Grant Thornton. 2020. https://www.grantthornton.global/globalassets/1.-member-firms/global/insights/women-in-business/2020/women-in-business-2020_report.pdf.

Jackson, Liam. "Adult learner fulfills lifelong goal, shares experiences through online program." Penn State News. June 13, 2017. https://news.psu.edu/story/471559/2017/06/13/academics/adult-learner-fulfills-lifelong-goal-shares-experiences-through.

Chapter 6

"Technical Writers." Occupational Outlook Handbook. U.S. Bureau of Labor Statistics. Modified September 21, 2020. https://www.bls.gov/ooh/media-and-communication/technical-writers.htm.

Chapter 8

"Jeremiah 29 - New International Version." Jeremiah 29:11. Biblica.com. https://www.biblica.com/bible/niv/jeremiah/29/.

"J.K. Rowling and the Billion-Dollar Empire." Forbes. February 26, 2004. https://www.forbes.com/2004/02/26/cx_jw_0226rowlingbill04.html#23c247636ce7.

Chapter 9

Updike, John. *Rabbit Redux*. Random House Trade Paperbacks. August 27, 1996.

Pofeldt, Elaine. "Full-time Freelancing Lures More Americans." Forbes. October 5, 2019. https://www.forbes.com/sites/elainepofeldt/2019/10/05/full-time-freelancing-lures-more-americans/#2c7239027259.

"Direct Selling in the United States: 2019 Industry Overview." PDF. Direct Selling Association. https://www.dsa.org/docs/default-source/research/growth-outlook/2019-research-overview-fact-sheet-final.pdf?sfvrsn=3bfedda5_2%27.

Kochhar, Rakesh. "Unemployment rose higher in three months of COVID-19 than it did in two years of the Great Recession." Pew Research Center. June 11, 2020. https://www.pewresearch.org/fact-tank/2020/06/11/unemployment-rose-higher-in-three-months-of-covid-19-than-it-did-in-two-years-of-the-great-recession/.

Chapter 10

Stallard, Michael Lee. "How U2's extraordinary team culture helps the band thrive." SmartBrief: Industry News. November 27, 2017. https://

www.smartbrief.com/original/2017/11/
how-u2s-extraordinary-team-culture-helps-band-thrive.

Vozza, Stephanie. "Personal Mission Statements Of 5 CEOs (And Why You Should Write One Too.) Fast Company. February 5, 2014. https://www.fastcompany. com/3026791/personal-mission-statements-of-5-famous-ceos-and-why-you-should-write-one-too.

Stillman, Jessica. "Richard Branson's 5-Step Process for Setting Goals (and Resolutions) You'll Actually Stick To." Inc.com. January 8, 2020. https://www.inc.com/jessica-stillman/richard-bransons-5-step-process-for-setting-goals-and-resolutions-youll-actually-stick-to.html.

Neustadt, Romi. *Get Over Your Damn Self: The No-BS Blueprint to Building a Life-Changing Business.* LiveFullOut Media. 2016.

Gallo, Carmine. "How Starbucks CEO Howard Schultz Inspired Us To Dream Bigger." Forbes. December 2, 2016. https://www.forbes.com/sites/ carminegallo/2016/12/02/how-starbucks-ceo-howard-schultz-inspired-us-to-dream-bigger/#6c7cd3c6e858.

Gregory, Lawrence. "Starbucks Coffee's Mission Statement & Vision Statement (An Analysis)." Panmore Institute. Updated February 16, 2019. http://panmore.com/ starbucks-coffee-vision-statement-mission-statement.

"Expect more than coffee." Starbucks.com. Culture and Values. https://www.starbucks.com/careers/ working-at-starbucks/culture-and-values.

"What is a SMART Goal?" Corporate Finance Institute. https://corporatefinanceinstitute.com/resources/ knowledge/other/smart-goal/.

Chapter 13

Bridges, Jeff and Matt Damon. *True Grit*. Directed by Ethan and Joel Cohen. Hollywood, CA: Paramount Pictures, 2010.

Chapter 14

Byrne, Rhonda. *The Secret*. Beyond Words Publishing. 2006.

Hicks, Esther and Jerry Hicks. *The Law of Attraction: The Basics of the Teachings of Abraham*. Hay House, Inc. 2006.

Hargreaves, Roger. *Mr. Happy*. Grosset & Dunlap. 1997.

Urban Manifestation. "What is the Law of Attraction? How to Make it Work for You?" Thrive Global. April 18, 2020. https://thriveglobal.com/stories/what-is-the-law-of-attraction-how-to-make-it-work-for-you/#:~:text=In%201877%2C%20the%20term%20%E2%80%9CLaw,Russian%20occultist%20Helena%20Petrovna%20Blavatsky.&text=She%20was%20the%20first%20person,and%20guided%20from%20within%20outwards.%E2%80%9D.

Chapter 15

Cohen, G. L. and D.K. Sherman. "The Psychology of Change: Self-Affirmation and Social Psychological Intervention." Annual Review of Psychology. PDF. 2014. https://www.annualreviews.org/doi/pdf/10.1146/annurev-psych-010213-115137#article-denial.

Hanscom, David. "Affirmations and Neuroplasticity." Psychology Today. January 30, 2020. https://www.psychologytoday.com/us/blog/anxiety-another-name-pain/202001/affirmations-and-neuroplasticity.

Rampton, John. "Neuroscience Tells Us How to Hack Our Brains for Success." Entrepreneur.com. June 16, 2017. https://www.entrepreneur.com/article/295885.

Chapter 16

"Micronutrient Facts." Centers for Disease Control and Prevention. CDC.gov. Last reviewed December 3, 2020. https://www.cdc.gov/nutrition/micronutrient-malnutrition/micronutrients/index.html.

"The Benefits of Eating Breakfast." WebMD. Reviewed December 27, 2018. https://www.webmd.com/diet/features/many-benefits-breakfast#4.

Zelman, Kathleen. "Diet Truth or Myth: Eating at Night Causes Weight Gain." WebMD. https://www.webmd.com/diet/features/diet-truth-myth-eating-night-causes-weight-gain#1.

"The Water in You: Water and the Human Body." USGS Water Science School. https://www.usgs.gov/special-topic/water-science-school/science/water-you-water-and-human-body?qt-science_center_objects=0#qt-science_center_objects.

Mayo Clinic Staff. "Exercise and stress : Get moving to manage stress." Mayo Foundation for Medical Education and Research. MayoClinic.org. August 18, 2020. https://www.mayoclinic.org/healthy-lifestyle/stress-management/in-depth/exercise-and-stress/art-20044469.

Pikul, Corrie. "Why Hitting The Snooze Button Will Screw Up Your Entire Day." Huffington Post. HuffPost.com. Updated December 6, 2017. https://www.huffpost.com/entry/why-hitting-snooze-is-bad-for-health_n_5630707.

Brandpoint. "4 tips for a happier gut and a healthier you." AP News. March 20, 2019. https://apnews.com/a18e644abb994b3ca76211179751129b.

Chapter 17

Lu, Stacy. "An Epidemic of Fear." American Psychological Association. APA.org. March 2015. https://www.apa.org/monitor/2015/03/fear.

Good Morning America. "Goldie Hawn Reveals Her Secret to Happiness." YouTube video, 3:23. May 30, 2016. https://www.youtube.com/watch?v=tiv2Bqz2VlE.

Chapter 19

"New Study Reveals How Long New Year's Resolutions Usually Last." CBS Philly. February 9, 2016. https://philadelphia.cbslocal.com/2016/02/09/new-study-reveals-how-long-new-years-resolutions-usually-last/.

"Dietary Supplements for Weight Loss." U.S. Department of Health and Human Services. National Institutes of Health. NIH.gov. Updated April 6, 2020. https://ods.od.nih.gov/factsheets/WeightLoss-HealthProfessional/#ref/.

Dean, Jeremy. "How Long to Form a Habit?" PsyBlog. Spring.org.uk. https://www.spring.org.uk/2009/09/how-long-to-form-a-habit.php.

Chapter 20

"Steve Jobs Biography." Biography.com. Updated June 10, 2020. https://www.biography.com/business-figure/steve-jobs.

The Editors of Encyclopaedia Britannica. "Oprah Winfrey." Encyclopaedia Britannica. Lat updated January 25, 2021. https://www.britannica.com/biography/Oprah-Winfrey.

Chapter 21

Bryant, Justin. "Jim Rohn Quotes That Inspire." SelfMadeSuccess.com. February 12, 2014. https://selfmadesuccess.com/jim-rohn-quotes/.

Price, Rob. "1 in 3 people check smartphones in the middle of the night." Insider.com. September 26, 2016. https://www.insider.com/1-in-3-people-check-smartphones-night-deloitte-study-2016-9.

Living Your Dream

Amadeo, Kimberly. "Unemployment Rate by Year Since 1929 Compared to Inflation and GDP." TheBalance.com. Updated September 17, 2020. https://www.thebalance.com/unemployment-rate-by-year-3305506.

Arruda, William. "6 Trends That Will Shape The Gig Economy In The 2020s." Forbes. https://www.forbes.com/sites/williamarruda/2020/07/12/6-trends-that-will-shape-the-gig-economy-in-the-2020s/#15d01b891565.

Clement, J. "Retail e-commerce sales in the United States from 2017 to 2024." Statista. 2021. https://www.statista.com/statistics/272391/us-retail-e-commerce-sales-forecast/.

Bedford, Emma. "Global Direct Selling Market: Statistics & Facts." Statista. March 30, 2020. https://www.statista.com/topics/4883/direct-selling-market/.

Hecht, Jared. "Are Small Businesses Really the Backbone of the Economy?" Inc.com. December 17, 2014.https://www.inc.com/jared-hecht/are-small-businesses-really-the-backbone-of-the-economy.html.

Chokshi, J. "Out of the Office: More People Are Working Remotely, Survey Finds." New York Times. February 15,

2017. https://www.nytimes.com/2017/02/15/us/remote-workers-work-from-home.html.

Harter, Jim. "How Coronavirus Will Change the 'Next Normal' Workplace." Gallup. May 1, 2020. https://www.gallup.com/workplace/309620/coronavirus-change-next-normal-workplace.aspx.

Acknowledgements ⦀

First, I am eternally grateful for my family, who love me for who I am, and who encourage and support me no matter what. I wouldn't be who and what I am without you. You mean the world to me.

I am grateful for my amazing circle of friends, who also love me for who I am and encourage and support me, but are willing to provide a kick in the pants when necessary. (You know who you are.)

I am grateful for Natasha and Rich Hazlett, who entered my life during a very difficult transition. I thought I was hiring Natasha as a business coach, but in reality, I found a life coach who truly helped me find my way back to the person I thought I'd lost. I am forever grateful to Natasha and Rich and the entire Unstoppable Influence community for encouraging me to share my message and live life by design—my design—at any age. Thanks in large part to them, I am unstoppable.

I am grateful for my brilliant editor, Julia Willson, who lovingly and expertly helped turn my manuscript into a much better book.

I am grateful for all the people I've met on my life journey. I have been blessed beyond belief to have the most amazing people in my life—the ones here and the ones who walk alongside and watch over me as guardian angels. You influence and inspire me every single day.

My husband once asked a dear friend to explain our purpose in life. Without hesitation, he said, "We're here to be kind to one another, to be good to one another, and to love one another." I appreciate the kindness, goodness, and love we've shared.

And finally, I'm grateful for all the canine family members I've had over the years who have provided unconditional love and companionship. We don't always understand each other, but that doesn't seem to matter. Maybe that's an important lesson in life.

About The Author |||

C hristine Stallard helps people rekindle their flame, master their mind, dare to dream, design a new path, and unleash their entrepreneurial spirit. In the process, they gain confidence and clarity to transition to an inspired life filled with passion and purpose, on their own terms and in any chapter.

Christine spent over 30 years in various government/public affairs positions in the corporate world and as a consultant where she communicated and educated the general public and policymakers on electric utility and natural resource issues. She coached and mentored employees, coworkers, and friends to help them reach their personal and professional goals.

Christine is an entrepreneur, author, life-long learner, avid college football fan (Penn State), lover of hot, spicy food, quilter, and (rather poor) pianist. She lives in the majestic Pacific Northwest with her husband and Bouvier des Flandres, and loves being surrounded by family, friends, and positive, fun-loving people.

You can learn more about Christine at christinestallard.com and join the conversation on social media at:

- Facebook: ChristineStallard.com/FB
- LinkedIn: ChristineStallard.com/LI

Here's Your Next Step... ‖

*L*ife is an amazing journey—a story with chapters and pages that are unique to each of us. Each one matters.

Now that you've read the book and completed the exercises, you're revved up and raring to go. It's time to put all that momentum into action so you get the confidence and clarity to dream, design, and live a chapter that's better than you ever imagined.

You're excited and inspired, but as Mary Morrissey says, "Inspiration without action is merely entertainment." Don't let all your dreams and the work you've done so far end up on the shelf.

I've developed additional tools that can help you on your journey. If you'd like to dive deeper into your Zone of Genius, take the quiz on my website at christinestallard.com. It's free!

If you'd like to learn more about additional programs and opportunities to work with me, go to christinestallard.com/programs.

Time is going to pass whether you're working on your dreams or not. You have to do the things that scare you, that push you outside your comfort zone. That's how you'll prove to yourself that you are stronger and more powerful than you thought.

I can't wait to hear all about your journey to your next, best chapter.